Dewey's Dream

Dewey's Dream

Universities and Democracies in
an Age of Education Reform

Civil Society, Public Schools,
and Democratic Citizenship

Lee Benson, Ira Harkavy,
and John Puckett

TEMPLE UNIVERSITY PRESS
Philadelphia

Temple University Press
1601 North Broad Street
Philadelphia PA 19122
www.temple.edu/tempress

⊗ The paper used in this publication meets the requirements of the American
National Standard for Information Sciences—Permanence of Paper for Printed
Library Materials, ANSI Z39.48–1992

Library of Congress Cataloging-in-Publication Data

Benson, Lee.
  Dewey's dream : universities and democracies in an age of education reform
civil society, public schools, and democratic citizenship / Lee Benson, Ira
Harkavy, and John Puckett.
     p. cm.
  Includes bibliographical references and index.
   ISBN-13: 978-1-59213-591-2   ISBN-10: 1-59213-591-9 (cloth : alk. paper)
   ISBN-13: 978-1-59213-592-9   ISBN-10: 1-59213-592-7 (pbk. : alk. paper)
     1. Dewey, John, 1859-1952. 2. Education—Philosophy. 3. Educational
change. I. Harkavy, Ira Richard. II. Puckett, John L., 1947- III. Title.
LB875.D5B46 2007
370.1—dc22   2006034208

  4 6 8 9 7 5 3

Contents

 Preface

Nothing is more conducive to innovation in social theory
than collaboration on a complex practical problem.

PAUL LAZARSFELD AND JEFFREY G. REITZ, *AN*
INTRODUCTION TO APPLIED SOCIOLOGY (1975)

THIS BOOK is not a traditional scholarly work. It is a democratic manifesto designed to help transform America into a truly participatory democracy—the model "city on a hill" dedicated to realizing John Dewey's inspiring utopian vision of a worldwide, organic "Great Community" composed of truly participatory, democratic, collaborative, and interdependent societies.

To realize our own utopian goal, we pay homage to Dewey, though we do so critically and constructively. Stated in highly general terms, we try to do three main things:

1. We trace the complex process whereby Dewey developed his utopian (i.e., inspiring) vision of a global "Great Community" composed of participatory democratic societies living together peacefully and harmoniously.
2. We critically analyze Dewey's failure to specify and demonstrate empirically the practical means needed to realize his utopian vision.
3. We propose a possible solution in order to stimulate the development of a massive worldwide academic movement dedicated to solving the terribly hard, critically important problem Dewey failed to solve.

In proposing a possible solution to what can conveniently be identified as the "Dewey Problem," we cannot overemphasize that our primary purposes are agenda setting and movement initiating, not thesis proving. Put another way, we hope to stimulate the constructive criticism, creative counterproposals, serious sustained debate, and experimental action necessary for an interactive international network of academics to develop the practical means necessary to solve the Dewey Problem and to realize Dewey's inspiring vision of a global "Great Community." Among numerous other significant benefits, development of that participatory democratic movement, particularly if it succeeded fully, would powerfully support the core proposition of Dewey's general theory of societal progress and the advancement of knowledge and learning: participatory democracy constitutes the best means human beings have yet devised to help solve the terribly complex problems they inevitably confront while struggling to achieve long and happy lives.

We have made this book short, inexpensive, relatively jargon free—and highly controversial. To summarize, it aims to advance the extraordinarily important democratic work John Dewey began in 1888, democratic work that now literally constitutes a matter of life and death for all human beings.

Introduction: Dewey's Lifelong Crusade for Participatory Democracy

It is not possible to run a course aright when the goal itself is not rightly placed.

FRANCIS BACON, *NOVUM ORGANON* (1620)

The true starting point of history is always some present situation with its problems.

JOHN DEWEY, *DEMOCRACY AND EDUCATION* (1916)

Democracy must begin at home, and its home is the neighborly community.

JOHN DEWEY, *THE PUBLIC AND ITS PROBLEMS* (1927)

I N THE RAPIDLY ACCELERATING GLOBAL ERA in which we now live, human beings must solve a vast array of unprecedently complex problems. Perhaps the most complex and most frightening problem is, what is to be done to prevent the possibility of a world perpetually terrorized by suicidal fanatics capable of acquiring and using scientifically and technologically advanced weapons of mass destruction to produce horrors instantly experienced by a worldwide audience? Given the proclaimed dedication of universities to critical intelligence, and their unique constellation of formidable resources to develop it, academics, we submit, have a unique responsibility to help solve that problem—indeed all the problems intensified by globalization.

To cope with the perilous situation we now confront in our radically different world, our more or less continued adherence to

Cardinal John Henry Newman's nineteenth-century elitist *Idea of a University* as a classical Ivory Tower in which British schoolboys could be ritualistically transformed into British "gentlemen" is dangerously anachronistic and dysfunctional. But what should replace it? Almost everywhere in the "developed" world, academics, to varying degrees, are grappling with that difficult problem. The best way to begin to solve it, we contend, is for academics to accept the general theory John Dewey proposed in 1888: participatory democracy "approaches most nearly the ideal of all social organization; that in which the individual and society are organic to each other."[1]

The strategy we propose for university and societal transformation is based on the assumption that Dewey was right: participatory democracy *is* the form of human society that would best enable all human beings to lead long, healthy, active, peaceful, virtuous, happy lives. Accordingly, to help solve the awesome problems confronting humanity in the twenty-first century, the highest priority of democratically minded academics in all developed societies should be helping their own communities and nations create the truly democratic society that Dewey envisioned as necessary if the world were to be transformed into a "Great Community," an integrated world of interactive, interdependent, truly collaborative, truly democratic societies. *Realizing that goal should receive the degree of desperate urgency given the Manhattan Project during World War II.*

During his unusually long lifetime, Dewey made an unusually wide range of theoretical contributions to human knowledge and societal progress. According to Robert Westbrook, one of his most insightful biographers, Dewey's lifelong efforts to advance participatory democracy constituted his most important theoretical contribution. The following is Professor Westbrook's elegant assessment of Dewey's work:

> Among liberal intellectuals of the twentieth century, Dewey was the most important advocate of participatory democracy, that is, of the belief that democracy, as an ethical ideal, calls upon men and women to build communities in which the necessary opportunities and resources are available for every

individual to realize fully his or her particular capacities and powers through participation in political, social, and cultural life. This ideal rested on a "faith in the capacity of human beings for intelligent judgment and action if proper conditions are furnished," a faith Dewey argued, "so deeply embedded in the methods which are intrinsic to democracy that when a professed democrat denies the faith he convicts himself of treachery to his profession."[2]

Westbrook views Dewey as the most important advocate of participatory democracy. But he acknowledges that Dewey never actually developed, let alone implemented, a comprehensive strategy capable of realizing his general theories in real-world practice. Following Westbrook's lead, in this book we pay homage to Dewey by trying to transcend him. By trying to transcend him, we mean reflectively building on both his general theories and his empirical experiments in order to solve what we call the *Dewey Problem*. What we mean by the Dewey Problem is, what *specifically is to be done beyond theoretical advocacy to transform American society and other developed societies into participatory democracies capable of helping to transform the world into a "Great Community"?*

As Dewey's lifelong failure to solve it demonstrates, the Dewey Problem is an extremely difficult problem. Precisely for that reason, in a world increasingly suffering from a growing array of horrors manifesting themselves daily, we contend that developing possible solutions to the Dewey Problem should now constitute the highest priority for democratically minded academics throughout the world. Since 1985, we and our colleagues across the United States and elsewhere in the world have been working to do so by developing the concept of "university-assisted community schools" (defined below) *and* by effectively creating national and international organizations to realize that concept in real-world practice. University-assisted community schools, in our judgment, constitute the best practical means to help realize Dewey's general theory of participatory democracy.

In later chapters, we will show *why* we believe that university-assisted community schools constitute the best practical means yet devised to realize Dewey's utopian ends and *how* they can best be developed. To provide the theoretical basis of our argument, we begin with a somewhat detailed exposition and critique of Dewey's own changing attempts to solve the Dewey Problem.

 Part I

Michigan Beginnings, 1884–1894

Democracy is not in reality what it is in name until it is industrial, as well as civil and political.

JOHN DEWEY, *THE ETHICS OF DEMOCRACY* (1888)

I N 1884 DEWEY COMPLETED graduate work in philosophy at Johns Hopkins University and began teaching at the University of Michigan. A committed Christian and Hegelian philosopher, he had little interest in societal theory or problems of democracy. By 1888, however, his interests and orientation had changed radically.

For a complex set of personal and intellectual reasons, which were probably influenced by the social and ideological conflicts then angrily dividing American society, Dewey enthusiastically advocated a new social theory. It was based on the "neo-Hegelian understanding of society as a peculiar kind of moral organism and the related notion of individual freedom within this organic society as the positive freedom to make the best of oneself as a social being and not merely the negative freedom from external restraint or compulsion."[1]

Having been converted during the mid-1880s to a participatory democratic theory of organic society based on the positive interaction between the common good and individual self-development, in 1888 Dewey published his long essay "The Ethics of Democracy." To present and support his own views, Dewey formed his essay into a sharp critique of Sir Henry Maine's influential denunciation of democracy in *Popular Government* (1885). Echoing ancient Greek and modern

attacks on democracy as inherently unstable, destructive, and anar-
chic, Maine insisted that democracy was "incapable, short of dema-
goguery or corruption, of generating the consensus essential to
effective government."[2] To refute Maine, Dewey forcefully argued
that the contrary was true.[3]

> In conception, at least, democracy approaches most nearly the
> ideal of all social organization; that in which the individual and
> society are organic to each other. For this reason democracy,
> so far as it is really democracy, is the most stable, not the most
> insecure, of governments. In every other form of government
> there are individuals who are not organs of the common will,
> who are outside of the political society in which they live, and
> are, in effect, aliens to that which should be their own com-
> monwealth. Not participating in the formation or expression
> of the common will, they do not embody it in themselves.
> Having no share in society, society has none in them.[4]

As the quotation demonstrates, Dewey theorized that only participatory democracy could produce the uncoerced, truly harmonious,
organic society most conducive to both the common good and to
individual self-development. A society governed by a participatory
democratic system of authoritative decision making, Dewey claimed,
is truly democratic precisely because all individuals freely and
actively participate "in the formation or expression of the common
will." They "embody it in themselves," feel that they have a "share in
society," are not alienated from other individuals, and actively function as full members of "their own commonwealth." Only uncoerced,
meaningful, universal, active participation in authoritative decision
making, Dewey flatly declared, can produce fundamental societal
harmony and cohesion, full-hearted devotion to the common good,
and continuous self-development and self-realization.

Dewey's glowing account of democracy as approaching "most
nearly the ideal [form] of all social organization" was, of course, completely theoretical. That is, to counter Maine's traditional empirical
claims that the "establishment of the masses in power" invariably

produces disastrous governmental and societal consequences, Dewey resorted to general observations about how a democratic government would, if it were truly democratic, work in theory. Nonetheless, in the process of refuting Maine, Dewey radically broadened democratic theory.

To strengthen his critique of Maine, Dewey declared that we cannot "stop with the idea of democracy as merely a form of government." Democracy, he passionately proclaimed, is much more than that; it "is a social, that is to say, an ethical conception and upon its ethical significance is based its significance as governmental."

> James Russell Lowell is a man of letters, not a professed student of politics and yet where he says of democracy that he is "speaking of a sentiment, a spirit, and not of a form of government . . .," we must recognize that the weight of history and of politics is on his side, as it is not on that of Maine.[5]

In 1888 Dewey did not yet explicitly characterize democracy as "a way of life," the all-inclusive phrase he used in later writings, but to refute Maine's criticism of democracy as entailing a type of "equality" that necessarily worked against human progress, Dewey invoked a radically antiaristocratic, comprehensive conception of equality and democracy. To support his argument, he again cited Lowell. Contrary to Maine,

> the true meaning of equality is synonymous with the definition of democracy given by James Russell Lowell. It is the form of society in which every man has a chance and knows that he has it—and we may add, a chance to which no possible limits can be put, a chance which is infinite, the chance to become a person. Equality, in short, is the ideal of humanity; an ideal in the consciousness of which democracy lives and moves.[6]

However, Dewey theorized that for a society to exist in which every individual has an equal chance and knows that he has it, democracy eventually must mean much more than political democracy. He writes, "There is no need to beat about the bush in saying that democracy is not in reality what it is in name *until it is industrial, as well as civil and political* [emphasis added]."[7]

As Westbrook observes, given the pressures and penalties to which "radical" American academics were then subjected, it was understandably prudent of Dewey to "not define carefully what he meant by industrial democracy."[8] For our present purposes, the critical point is that Dewey's deliberately vague call in 1888 for industrial democracy radically extended "democracy" to mean much more than simply a form of government. In later writings, when Dewey felt much more secure than he did in 1888, he unequivocally asserted that for democracy truly to be democracy, it had to be conceived as a highly inclusive form of societal organization comprehending "all modes of human association."

As noted above, Dewey's strong defense and advocacy of participatory democracy was completely theoretical. That is, in his 1888 "Democratic Manifesto" (our term for "The Ethics of Democracy"), he made no attempt to show that as democracy then functioned in the United States (or anywhere else) it bore anything more than a superficial resemblance to his highly idealized conception of how it should and would work. Among other rhetorical advantages, by restricting himself to theoretical arguments, he avoided having to answer a whole set of very difficult questions. Among them are the following:

- What empirical evidence existed that Dewey's idealized "conception" of participatory democracy represented anything but wishful thinking directly contrary to human nature and, therefore, impossible to realize in practice?
- If his conception of democracy could potentially be realized in practice, why hadn't it been; why did nothing resembling it actually exist?
- What *specifically* did such noble-sounding phrases as "participating in the formation or expression of the common will" and "shar[ing] in society" really mean?
- What resources must individuals possess to participate, and feel that they can participate, in the "formation or

expression of the common will" and actually have a "share in society?"

- What specific institutional arrangements and processes were necessary to produce genuinely democratic participation in governmental and societal decision making?
- Was the legal right to vote in elections for governmental officials and formal specifications of civil liberties in the First Amendment to the U.S. Constitution enough to realize participatory democracy in practice? If they were not, what other institutional arrangements, conditions, and processes were necessary?
- Most importantly, if the comprehensive set of institutional arrangements, conditions, and processes needed to realize Dewey's conception of participatory democracy did not then exist in the United States (or anywhere else), what specifically could and should be done to develop and effectively implement them and by whom? How did Dewey *specifically* propose to get there (participatory democracy) from here (existing state of U.S. political and societal systems)?

In 1888 Dewey made no attempt to convincingly answer any of these extraordinarily difficult questions. Viewed in historical perspective, however, his essay contributed significantly to the advance of democracy. It did so by both radically broadening the conception of democracy and by implicitly raising the set of critical questions listed above. "The Ethics of Democracy" essay provided a highly constructive agenda for Dewey's subsequent work, as well as for the work of the innumerable advocates of democracy whom he subsequently influenced, both directly and indirectly.

Dewey's First Attempt to Combine Theory and Practice

Soon after his "Ethics of Democracy" essay was published, Dewey recognized that to advance participatory democracy he had to do much more than present theoretical arguments—he had to explicitly combine theory and practice. He became convinced that real-world action was mandatory if he were to function as more than a "Scholastic" in an academic monastery who merely criticized "the criticisms with which some other Scholastic has criticized other criticisms, and the writings upon writings goes on till the substructure of reality is long abused."[9] Given his "intense desire to escape from a cloistered academic routine" and "eager[ness] to spread his ideas beyond the classroom," from 1888 to 1892 Dewey worked increasingly with an experienced crusading journalist named Franklin Ford.[10] Westbrook's summary of Ford's grandiose utopian plan to advance democracy in America is very clear:

> Ford was a minor prophet among late nineteenth century American utopians, an ideological cousin of Henry George and Edward Bellamy, but unlike them he was interested less in the control of the means of production than in control of the means of communication. His vision rested on a belief that the key to social justice in America was a radical reorganization of the production and distribution of knowledge. The reformer's task was one of freeing the American people, whom Ford referred to as the "Representative Slaves," from the "class interest which found its profit in keeping the common fact covered up." Progress toward a cooperative commonwealth rested on the "socialization of intelligence." The agency for this reconstruction of society was to be a powerful corporation that Ford called the "Intelligence Trust." This trust—an organization of intellectuals and journalists—would create a giant central clearinghouse of information and analysis, and through its own publications and the material it sold to newspapers throughout the country it would provide the public with the knowledge it needed to free itself from slavery. By making the truth its business, the Intelligence Trust would put publications serving class interests out of business. "In place of discussing 'socialism,'" Ford said, "we put out in the rightful sense of the word, the socialistic newspaper—the organ of the whole."[11]

Dewey at first responded cautiously to Ford's utopian idea that the creation of a "giant central clearinghouse of information" could transform America into the kind of organic society he had theoretically envisioned in his 1888 essay. Within a year or two of meeting Ford, however, according to Neil Coughlan (another insightful Dewey biographer), he became much more enthusiastic and began to blame America's troubles on the "state of intelligence on its thought side."[12] Like Ford, Dewey concluded that "it was principally a deficit of intelligence that stood between America and the good society. 'Intelligence,' that is, 'news,' was Ford's, the reporter's business; but after all, wasn't 'intelligence,' that is 'mind,' his own, Dewey's business? He was entranced."[13] There is no need to recite the details of the complex process by which Dewey convinced himself that the visionary journalist had solved the Hegelian problem of transforming society into a "systematic, organic whole" by constructing an "Intelligence Trust" powerful enough to make "information, 'intelligence' . . . now . . . universally and instantaneously available." The point is that, as Coughlan notes, "Dewey mulled and puzzled over Ford's meanings and implications for three years and then, in 1891, prepared to throw aside the caution of a closet utopian and proclaim publicly that these were world-historic times."[14]

Working together, the Hegelian professor and the professional newspaperman would "fulfill the promise of the age." How would they do that? How would they "reveal the meaning of the age" to the world and, therefore, help change it radically for the better?

Their vehicle would be a newspaper, *Thought News*, "a journal of inquiry and a record of fact." Ford and Dewey appear to have worked on the plans for their paper all that fall and winter [1891–1892], and Dewey's actual scholarly output dropped off to almost nothing. . . . Early in March 1892, as the publication date for the first issue of the journal bore down on him, he wrote to . . . a former student of his about his dreams for *philosophy and action* [emphasis added]. His letter concluded, "These things would sound more or less crazy to a professor of philosophy in good and regular standing, but I intend henceforth to act on my conviction regardless. Hence, among other things, *Thought News*."[15]

Soon after writing that letter, Dewey prepared a circular announcing that the "first number of the *Thought News*" would appear in April 1892. He published the circular in the March 16 issue of the University of Michigan's student newspaper, the *Michigan Daily*, in which he proclaimed how and why *Thought News* would differ from all other newspapers and magazines of the time. Moreover, Dewey's circular explicitly noted, "The immediate responsibility for its conduct will be in the hands of John Dewey of the philosophical department of the University of Michigan. The need of the paper lies in the present condition of intelligence on the thought side. The enterprise is prompted by an inquiry movement centering in Ann Arbor."[16] Despite Dewey's bold proclamation, no issue of *Thought News* ever appeared.

Soon after his circular was published in the *Michigan Daily*, the paper printed another statement: it announced that the first issue of *Thought News* would appear "on or about April 22." The statement was unsigned, but Neil Coughlan attributes it to Franklin Ford and observes that it made such extravagant claims on behalf of the epoch-making significance of *Thought News* that Dewey was quickly and repeatedly subjected to withering ridicule and criticism by the *Detroit Tribune*. Devastated by the public ridicule and criticism to which he had subjected himself, Dewey quarreled with Ford, beat an ignominious retreat, and allowed the project, which he had energetically and enthusiastically worked on for four years, to disappear into oblivion.[17]

To Coughlan, the primary meaning of the *Thought News* fiasco was its demonstration that Dewey "had a lifelong weakness for quacks" and their crackpot schemes.[18] Probably because Westbrook strongly supports Dewey's evolving general theory of participatory democracy, he presents a significantly different—and much more flattering—interpretation of the episode. He regards Ford as a highly innovative thinker who perceptively recognized a very important societal development, namely, that the increasingly centralized control of communication media functioned to develop a "societal structure that prevented freedom of inquiry" and seriously lessened the possibility of democracy. In Westbrook's view, therefore, Ford not only significantly helped Dewey see the significance of that development, his scheme also struck Dewey as a practical plan for creating an essential condition of participatory democracy.

If participatory democracy were ever to be realized, Dewey now theorized, it was mandatory that freedom of inquiry and information exist on an increasingly universal scale and that a practical means be developed to make the necessary "intelligence" easily available to all members of society. In principle, modern technological changes in communication were making that condition possible. As Westbrook interprets the Dewey-Ford episode, what Ford proposed was critically important if an organic society and participatory democracy were ever to develop. Summarized succinctly, Ford proposed that Dewey and he radically challenge and overcome the existing social structure, take advantage of the technological revolution occurring in communication, and thereby help bring about the "socialized intelligence" Dewey believed to be mandatory to achieve a "Good Society" (which he later extended and called the worldwide "Great Community"). In Westbrook's view, that is why Dewey responded so enthusiastically to Ford's radical ideas and why Ford played such "an important role in the development of Dewey's social philosophy"—so important, in fact, that "it was Ford, more than anyone else, who in the early 1890s directed . . . [Dewey's] turn toward radical democracy."[19] Obviously their emphases differ but the interpretations and insights of Coughlan and Westbrook are not inherently contradictory. For us, however, the most revealing aspects of the *Thought News* episode can be summarized as follows.

On the one hand, participation in the *Thought News* project helped Dewey recognize that, by itself, academic theory could not advance societal progress. To help achieve desirable societal ends, general theories had to be "instrumentally" combined with practical reason (i.e., strategic practical means). Otherwise, academic theories almost invariably functioned as utopian theories, in the pejorative sense of the word. From then on, Dewey preached the unity of scientific theory *and* practice, the unity of intelligence *and* action.

On the other hand, the *Thought News* project powerfully illumi-
nated Dewey's habitual aversion to the highly intensive, genuinely
"scientific" study of the societal problems that he passionately
wanted to solve, as well as his lifelong resistance to doing the hard,
sustained, *practical* thinking and work necessary to solve those problems in any realistic way. As Ellen Lagemann has forcefully observed,

> However appealing John Dewey's thought may be, there is no
> denying that it lacks a sense of real politick. Dewey's descrip-
> tion of democracy as associated living, of schools as embry-
> onic communities, and of politics as the education of publics
> have stirred the imagination of many people because they
> resonate with deeply humane and widely shared values . . . .
> Despite that, when one reads Dewey's writings wanting to
> know how the kind of democracy, education, or politics he
> described might be developed, one comes up lacking.[20]

Consider the grandiose functions *Thought News* was designed to
perform and the resources actually available to establish, support,
and maintain the paper. How could the young, underpaid and over-
worked chairman of the minuscule Department of Philosophy at the
provincial University of Michigan, in the provincial town of Ann
Arbor, possibly have been able to create, finance, and operate a newspaper circulated so widely that it would function as a "giant central
clearinghouse of information"—a vast repository capable of competing with, and effectively countering, the exponentially growing commercial media that increasingly dominated the national
communication system? To pose the question is to answer it; but posing the question reveals and underscores the astonishingly illogical,
delusionary, utopian character of the plan that Ford and Dewey had
fantasized they could put into practice. Critically examined, we contend, Dewey's participation in the *Thought News* project helps illu-
minate both his strengths and weaknesses, and, as we will try to show
in Chapter 2, why he benefited so greatly from leaving Michigan for
Chicago in 1894.

2 Dewey at the University of Chicago, 1894–1904

Democracy has been given a mission to the world, and it is of no uncertain character. I wish to show that the university is the prophet of this democracy, as well as its priest and philosopher; that in other words, the university is the Messiah of the democracy, its to-be-expected deliverer.

WILLIAM RAINEY HARPER,
"THE UNIVERSITY AND DEMOCRACY" (1899)

I F OUR PROPOSITIONS ARE NOT taken literally, John Dewey primarily became Dewey in Chicago and henceforth essentially lived off the intellectual capital he developed at that university and in that city. Obviously, we deliberately oversimplify and exaggerate to help make our basic point: Dewey's most important intellectual development took place in Chicago, and he did his most important work there. Though he never lost interest in the theory of communication that excited him so greatly at Michigan, it was not until he went to Chicago that he saw that the best strategy for developing a participatory democratic society was to develop a participatory democratic schooling system. To support that proposition, we begin by noting a tendency of previous scholarship to greatly exaggerate Dewey's interest and work in education before he came to Chicago in 1894 and after he left it for New York and Columbia University in 1904.

If we carefully examine all of Dewey's publications from 1882 to 1894 and do not anachronistically read into his Michigan years the great interest in pedagogy and schools he came to develop at the University of Chicago, it is clear that, at best, those subjects were of only minor interest to him at that time. In the four lengthy volumes for the Michigan years in the *Early Works of John Dewey, 1882–1898*, only a handful of very brief articles deal with education, and they focus on such highly specialized topics as "Education and the Health of Women," "Health and Sex in Higher Education," and "Psychology in High-Schools from the Standpoint of the College." As those titles indicate, his Michigan publications had little or nothing to do with the problems of pedagogy and schools that greatly engaged him at Chicago. Understandably, therefore, in his introduction to Dewey's *Early Works*, the editor of "Volume 4, 1893–1894" observes that Dewey was then "still a novice in . . . educational theory."[1]

At the risk of seeming to indulge in the academic game of one-upmanship, for reasons that will later become clear, we must point out that, contrary to erroneous accounts in various biographies, Dewey had nothing to do with establishing the Department of Pedagogy at the University of Chicago. Moreover, his appointment did not come about because of his interest or work in that subject. On the contrary, the available evidence seems conclusive that he was offered and accepted the appointment for entirely different reasons.

President Harper and Chicago's Department of Pedagogy

Even before the University of Chicago began formal operations in October 1892, its president, William Rainey Harper, "expressed some interest in establishing a school of pedagogy." At that time his primary motives were to attract students to the new university and to gain it support from wealthy Chicago elites who had become highly interested in improving the public schools of Chicago. Though his views changed radically soon after he created the Department of Pedagogy in 1892, Harper was then not very impressed with the utility of courses in pedagogy. In addition to his other motives for creating the Department of Pedagogy, it helped him recruit Julia E. Bulkley as the first dean of women at the university. Harper was very impressed with her organizational abilities, but "she insisted that her responsibilities at the university include work in education."[2]

Acceding to her demands, he appointed her to the rank of associate professor of pedagogy, gave her a leave of absence until 1895 to travel to Europe and secure a PhD, and staffed the Department of Pedagogy with a teaching fellow from the Department of Philosophy.[3]

As is well known, Dewey was not Harper's first choice for head of the philosophy department, and he owed his appointment to James H. Tufts, an assistant professor in that department who had been a colleague of Dewey's in Michigan. Aware that the vacancy existed, Tufts wrote a letter to Harper strongly recommending Dewey on a variety of grounds. None of these grounds had anything to do with pedagogy or schools, nor did any of the "more important publications of Professor Dewey" listed by Tufts to support his letter of recommendation.[4]

To our knowledge, no document exists that helps explain why Harper appointed Dewey as head of the Department of Pedagogy, which he had created in 1892, as well as head of the combined Department of Philosophy and Psychology. (Pedagogy and philosophy continued to be separate departments headed by Dewey for several years.) Harper may have done so to justify having acceded to Dewey's demand that his salary be $5,000 rather than the $4,000 originally offered him. Moreover, Julia Bulkley was still on leave in Europe, and by 1894 Harper's views on pedagogy had changed dramatically. He himself was now very actively engaged in the accelerating efforts to improve the Chicago public school system and wanted to strengthen his university's Department of Pedagogy. Appointing a prestigious full professor of philosophy to head it might achieve that goal and appeal to public school-minded city elites, as well. In short, Dewey's appointment as head of the Department of Pedagogy is best understood as resulting from a series of events in Chicago related to public schools that had transformed Harper's interest in education.

By the time Dewey arrived in Chicago in July 1894, Harper was playing a highly prominent role in the major campaign then underway by leading citizens and powerful civic groups to radically change public education in Chicago. Given Dewey's limited interest and work in education at Michigan, it seems clear to us that Harper's intense commitment to school reform, directly and indirectly, strongly influenced Dewey's ideas about education and society after he left provincial Ann Arbor and was, to quote Westbrook's perceptive observation, "thrust . . . into the maelstrom of the prototypical metropolis of industrializing America."[5]

To a much greater degree than has generally been recognized, we contend that Dewey's ideas about education and society benefited from the great importance President Harper placed upon his university's active engagement with the severe problems confronting its dynamically growing city—particularly its public school system. For example, criticized by a university trustee for sponsoring a journal focused on pedagogy in *precollegiate schools*, Harper emphatically proclaimed, "As a university we are interested above all else in pedagogy."[6] Harper's conversion to the centrality of pedagogy logically derived from two propositions central to his messianic vision for the University of Chicago in particular and American universities in general.[7]

1. "Education is the basis of all democratic progress. The problems of education are, therefore, the problems of democracy."[8]
2. More than any other institution, the university determines the character of the overall schooling system: "Through the school system, the character of which, in spite of itself, the university determines and in a large measure controls . . . through the school system every family in this entire broad land of ours is brought into touch with the university; for from it proceed the teachers or the teachers' teachers."[9]

Given those two propositions and the role Harper assigned the American university as the "to-be-expected deliverer" of American democracy, he theorized that the major responsibility of universities is the performance of the schooling system as a whole. If the American schooling system does not powerfully accelerate "democratic progress," then American universities must be performing poorly—no matter whatever else they are doing successfully. "By their democratic fruits shall ye know them," is the pragmatic performance test Harper, in effect, prescribed for the American university system.

Even before his appointment in 1890 as the first president of the University of Chicago (which formally did not begin operation until 1892), Harper had demonstrated remarkably innovative abilities in the teaching and organization of religious studies. A passionately dedicated and creative scholar, at an early age he had become the leading biblical authority in the United States. According to Harper biographer James P. Wind, "scholars in the emerging profession of Old Testament Studies looked to Harper as their dean." Harper not only passionately studied the Old Testament, his "fundamental vision" for the University of Chicago was inspired by it.[10] Wind writes,

> In the Hebrew Scriptures Harper found the raw material that provided the ground of his personal beliefs, the field of his professional competence and the *paradigm for reshaping education in America* [emphasis added]. Within those cherished texts, Harper discerned a God at work in history lifting humanity toward a still to be realized "higher life." The most fundamental idea of all for him was that God moves some to suffer vicariously for others. Israel suffered for the scattered nations; Jesus suffered for a fallen humanity; the biblical scholars struggled to provide new meaning for suffering moderns; and the university, in its grappling with the great problems of the ages, was called to suffer for society in order that all its members might ascend to higher life. Ultimately, Harper's vision was messianic. He traced the messianic idea from its prophetic origins up to its application in his day; indeed he could claim without batting an exegetical eye— that the university was "Messiah."[11]

Inspired by his messianic vision, Harper placed schools, universities in particular, at the strategic center of American intellectual and institution-building agendas. He made a seminally important theoretical contribution when he identified the university as the strategic institution capable of creating a truly democratic society. For Harper, the American university had a singular, "holy" purpose: to be the "prophet of democracy."[12] Indeed, no other university president so passionately and farsightedly envisioned the university's democratic potential and purpose. Profoundly religious and deeply dedicated to the progressive Social Gospel, Harper conceptualized the university as the holy place designed to fulfill democracy's creed: "the brotherhood, and consequently the equality of man."[13] The university would fulfill that creed through "service for mankind, wherever mankind is, whether within scholastic walls, or without these walls and in the world at large."[14]

In his 1899 essay "The University and Democracy," Harper presented his radical, antielitist, uniquely American idea of the university in powerful, moving language:

> The university, I contend, is this prophet of democracy—*the agency established by heaven itself to proclaim the principles of democracy* [emphasis added]. It is in the university that the best opportunity is afforded to investigate the movements of the past and to present the facts and principles involved before the public. It is the university that, as the center of thought, is to maintain for democracy the unity so essential for its success. *The university is the prophetic school out of which come the teachers who are to lead democracy in the true path* [emphasis added]. It is the university that must guide democracy into the new fields of arts and literature and science. It is the university that fights the battles of democracy, its war-cry being: "come, let us reason together." It is the university that, in these latter days, goes forth with buoyant spirit to comfort and give help to those who are downcast, *taking up its dwelling in the very midst of squalor and distress* [emphasis added]. It is the university that, with impartial judgment, condemns in democracy the spirit of corruption, which now and again lifts up its head, and brings scandal

upon democracy's fair name. . . . The university, I maintain, is the prophetic interpreter of democracy; the prophet of her past, in all its vicissitudes; the prophet of her present, in all its complexity; the prophet of her future, in all its possibilities.[15]

For Harper, the new urban university, in particular, would be the strategic agent to help America realize and fulfill its democratic promise. Other presidents (e.g., Daniel Coit Gilman of Johns Hopkins and Seth Low of Columbia) enthusiastically seized the opportunity to build their institutions by working to improve the quality of life in American cities. But Harper went much further than his presidential colleagues when he predicted that an institutional transformation—a positive mutation—would result if universities engaged in planned interaction with their urban environments. For example, speaking in 1902 at Nicholas Murray Butler's inauguration as president of Columbia University, Harper prophetically hailed the extraordinary intellectual and institutional advances that would come about when that planned interaction finally occurred.

A university which will adapt itself to urban influence, which will undertake to serve as an expression of urban civilization, and which is compelled to meet the demands of an urban environment, *will in the end become something essentially different from a university located in a village or small city* [emphasis added].[16]

In that same address, in effect, Harper invoked John Dewey's fundamental pragmatic proposition that major advances in knowledge strongly tend to occur when human beings consciously work to solve the central problems confronting their society. "The urban universities found today in . . . the largest cities in this country . . . and in [Europe]," Harper declaimed, "form a class by themselves, inasmuch as they are compelled to deal with problems which are not involved in the work of universities located in smaller cities. . . . Just as the great cities of the country represent the national life in its fullness and variety, so the urban universities are in the truest sense . . . national universities." To conclude his address, he proclaimed that of all the great institutions in New York City, Columbia University was "the greatest."[17] In Chicago, Harper certainly believed, his university held that preeminent position. Succinctly summarized, Harper's "messianic" thesis viewed *the university as the prime mover of modern democratic societies*.

During his ten years at Chicago, Dewey's work was powerfully influenced by Harper's vision, program, and wide-ranging activities both directly and indirectly. More specifically, the great importance Harper placed upon pedagogy and education helped Dewey see that the schooling system—*not* the communication system—was the strategic agency to help institute the participatory democratic society he had envisioned in 1888. Put another way, it was only after Dewey came to Chicago that he essentially adopted Plato's educational strategy as the best means to achieve the Good Participatory Democratic Society.

Plato's *The Republic* and Dewey's Philosophy of Education

Plato was the philosopher Dewey most liked to read. Though he admired Plato, their worldviews differed radically. We need only note two basic differences: Plato's worldview was aristocratic and contemplative, whereas Dewey's was democratic and activist. Despite their many differences, Dewey's immersion in the dynamic Chicago schooling environment led him to see the great value of the basic ideas Plato had developed in *The Republic* concerning the relationships between education and society. To summarize Dewey's views on education after 1894, we quote a leading philosopher of education, Steven M. Cahn. According to Cahn, Dewey believed that

> philosophy of education was the most significant phase of philosophy. Charles Frankel once noted that for Dewey "all philosophy was at bottom social philosophy implicitly or explicitly." I would extend this insight and suggest that for Dewey all social philosophy was at bottom philosophy of

education implicitly or explicitly. As he put it, "it would be difficult to find a single important problem of general philosophic inquiry that does not come to a burning focus in matters of the determination of the proper subject matter of studies, the choice of methods of teaching, and the problem of social organization and administration of the schools."[18]

Noting that other philosophers also emphasized the importance of education, Cahn quotes Kant's proposition that "the greatest and most difficult problem to which man can devote himself is the problem of education." Cahn then observes that he knows of

only two major philosophers who exemplified this principle in their philosophical work: one was Dewey, the other was Plato. He too found it difficult to discuss any important philosophical problem without reference to the appropriateness of various subjects of study, methods of teaching, or strategies of learning. But while Dewey's philosophy of education rested on his belief in democracy and the power of scientific method, Plato's philosophy of education rested on his belief in aristocracy and the power of pure reason. Plato proposed a planned society, Dewey a society engaged in continuous planning. Plato considered dialectical speculation to be the means toward the attainment of truth; Dewey maintained that knowledge is only acquired through intelligent action. . . . Suffice it to say that John Dewey is the only thinker ever to construct a philosophy of education comparable in scope and depth to that of Plato.[19]

Like the ancient Greek philosopher, after 1894 Dewey theorized that education and society were dynamically interactive and interdependent. It followed, therefore, that if human beings hope to develop and maintain a particular type of society or social order, they must develop and maintain the particular type of education system conducive to it—no effective democratic schooling system, no democratic society.

It is critically important to emphasize another radical difference between Plato and Dewey. To implement his aristocratic philosophy of education and society, Plato created what can arguably, if loosely, be viewed as the world's first university: the remarkably influential Academy, whose elitist, idealist philosophy of education continues to dominate Western schooling systems to this day. Surprisingly, Dewey never saw what Plato—and William Rainey Harper—saw so clearly: universities invariably constitute by far the most strategic component of a society's schooling system. Dewey's failure to see that had disastrous consequences. It resulted in his work on education giving remarkably little attention to the role of universities and therefore prevented him from ever developing the comprehensive strategy necessary to realize in practice the democratic system of "school and society" that he so passionately desired and so passionately preached.

Participatory Democratic Societies and Participatory Democratic Schooling Systems

Probably the clearest statement of Dewey's fundamental proposition that a participatory democratic society must be based on a participatory democratic schooling system is found in his 1897 essay "Ethical Principles Underlying Education."[20] Particularly when read in light of Dewey's role in the *Thought News* episode in Michigan, it seems clear that the essay was designed to solve the strategic problem he now knew had to be solved if participatory democracy were to be realized in practice, namely: What *practical means* could be developed and implemented to achieve his utopian theoretical end? More generally, what conditions had to be satisfied for all individuals to be capable of participating actively, effectively, and wholeheartedly in the authoritative decision-making processes of their community and society, and thereby realize their fullest personal development? Dewey's answer to this question was that a public schooling system would have to be developed that functioned in ways that provided a student with "training in science, in art, in history; command of the fundamental methods of inquiry and the fundamental tools of intercourse and communication, . . . a trained and sound body, skillful eye and hand, habits of industry, perseverance, and above all, habits of serviceableness." Moreover, for the student to be an active, effective member of a "democratic and progressive society," he "must be educated for leadership as well as for obedience. He must have power of self-direction and power of directing others, power of administration, ability to assume positions of responsibility. This necessity of educating for leadership is as great on the industrial as on the political side."[21] And since society is now—and in the future certainly will be—changing rapidly,

> it is an absolute impossibility to educate the . . . [student] for any fixed station in life. . . . [Thus] the ethical responsibility of the school on the social side must be interpreted in the broadest and freest spirit, . . . which will give him such possession of himself that he may take charge of himself; may not only adapt himself to the changes which are going on but have power to shape and direct those changes. . . . Apart from the thought of participation in social life the school has no end nor aim. . . . The fundamental conclusion is that the school must be made itself into a vital social institution to a very much greater extent than obtains at present. . . . Excepting in so far as the school is an embryonic yet typical community life, moral training must be . . . [severely deficient]. Interest in the community welfare, an interest which is intellectual and practical, as well as emotional—an interest, that is to say, in perceiving whatever makes for social order and progress, and for carrying these principles into execution—is the ultimate ethical habit to which all the special school habits must be related.[22]

By 1897, when Dewey published "Ethical Principles Underlying Education," he was deeply engaged in developing an elementary school at the University of Chicago. Though it was designed to aid the work of the Department of Pedagogy, and was therefore partially subsidized by the university, it essentially was a private school founded by Dewey and almost completely controlled by him. Appropriately enough, it quickly acquired the moniker the "Dewey School," which Dewey had conceived to function as a scientific laboratory to develop educational theories and empirical propositions that would radiate out from it and revolutionize the entire American schooling system. Therefore, the Dewey School soon came to be referred to as the "Laboratory School."[23]

Dewey's Laboratory School

Viewed in the larger perspective of the radical enterprise that Dewey had begun in 1888, it seems clear that Dewey's strategy once had been to institute participatory democracy in America by using the *Thought News* journal to revolutionize the American communication system. But by 1897 his strategy was to use the Laboratory School to revolutionize the American schooling system and thereby achieve his post-1888 "end-in-view." Though Dewey now worked in Chicago, his real goal, as in Ann Arbor, was democratizing American society.

Dewey discussed his educational ideas most fully in a volume published in 1899, *The School and Society*, a collection of essays drawn from the experience of the Dewey School. In *The School and Society*—the book that catapulted him into the role of world-famous educator—and in subsequent writings, Dewey sought to lead a crusade to radically transform, modernize, and democratize the American schooling system. In the process, he developed a general theory of instrumental intelligence derived from the following basic proposition:

Intelligence is not a fixed quality. Dewey theorized that intelligence, like speech, is an *innate capacity* human beings possess by virtue of their unique biological nature as *human* organisms. Human beings can powerfully develop their innate capacity for intelligence by using it *instrumentally* to solve the strategic problems that inevitably confront them from birth until death. Human beings best develop their innate capacity for intelligent thought and action when they purposefully use it as a powerful instrument to help them solve the multitude of perplexing problems that continually confront them in their daily lives—and when they reflect on their experience and thereby increase their capacity for *future* intelligent thought and action. Intelligence does not develop simply as a result of problem-solving action and experience; it develops best as a result of *reflective, strategic*, real-world problem-solving action and experience. Education is a powerful means human beings have evolved to develop their innate biological capacity to solve problems by thinking and acting purposefully, effectively, and reflectively. Dewey emphasized that action-oriented, collaborative, real-world problem-solving education can function as the most powerful means to raise the level of instrumental intelligence in individuals, groups, communities, societies, and humanity.

To a very great extent, Dewey's program to revolutionize the formal American schooling system derived intellectually from his highly romanticized analysis of the "preindustrial apprentice-like, household- and community-based, informal learning system" (our lengthy term for his central concept). In *The School and Society*, Dewey emphasized that in preindustrial society, "the household was practically the center in which were carried on, or about which were clustered, all the typical forms of industrial occupation." Goods that came from outside the household were

> produced in the immediate neighborhood in shops which were constantly open to inspection and often centers of neighborhood congregation. The entire industrial process stood revealed, from the production on the farm of the raw material til the finished article was actually put to use. Not only this, but practically every member of the household had his own share in the work. *The children, as they gained in strength and capacity, were gradually initiated into the mysteries of the several processes. It was a matter of immediate and personal concern, even to the point of actual participation* [emphasis added]. We cannot overlook the factors of discipline and of character-building involved in this kind of life: *training in habits of order and industry; and in the idea of responsibility,*

of obligation to do something, to produce something, in the world [emphasis added]. . . . Personalities which became effective in action were bred and tested in the medium of action. Again, we cannot overlook the importance for educational purposes of the close and immediate acquaintance got with nature at first hand, with real things and materials, with the actual processes of their manipulation, and the knowledge of their social necessities and uses. In all this there was continual training of observation, of ingenuity, constructive imagination, of logical thought, *and of the sense of reality acquired through first-hand contact with actualities* [emphasis added].[24]

Unfortunately, in organizing and developing his Laboratory School, Dewey failed to make good use of his brilliant, radically anti-idealist, real-world household and community problem-solving analysis of the educational benefits inherent in the informal, natural learning systems of preindustrial societies. On the contrary, his Laboratory School radically violated the real-world problem-solving educational principles essential to his analysis.

Dewey's idealized analysis of preindustrial "natural learning systems" (our term) provides the key, we believe, to his prescription for radical reform of the *formal* schooling system of twentieth-century American industrial society. He did not look backward simply to bemoan the loss of the preindustrial informal learning system that had produced the highly desirable qualities specified in the lengthy quotation above. Instead, as utopians do, he looked backward primarily to help bring about radical change in the existing formal schooling system. Dewey theorized that good modern schools would develop in children both the desirable qualities of *localistic*, parochial, preindustrial society, as well as the desirable qualities of the more *cosmopolitan*, liberal industrial society produced by the post-1800 economic and communication revolutions.

As noted above, Dewey disdained the almost entirely medieval formal schooling system that existed in 1899. It alarmed him that children increasingly were subjected to that system; he recognized that as factories replaced households as centers of production and as work became separate and distant from home and neighborhood, children were segregated in formal schools that isolated them from adults (other than teachers) and from participation in community activity. In a profound sense, he viewed existing American schools as unnatural institutions, contrary to human nature and daily community life. From his theory of human nature and his observations of children, Dewey concluded that children were naturally curious, eager to learn how to do things, and dynamically active. But when untutored, undirected, and undisciplined, their natural tendencies and instincts *did not* result in intellectual or moral development. Therefore, it followed that "the question of education is the question of taking hold of [the learner's] activities, of giving them direction. Through direction, through organized use, they tend toward valuable results, instead of scattering or being left to merely impulsive expression."[25]

In Dewey's analysis of prcindustrial society, daily life in the household and community imposed direction, organization, and discipline on children to produce the set of desirable qualities he described so glowingly. But preindustrial society was rapidly disappearing. As societies became more complex in structure and resources, "the school must now supply that factor of training formerly taken care of in the home."[26] That is, in industrial societies, to educate children so that they can most effectively develop their innate capacity for intelligent thought and action, formal schooling and learning must replace the informal learning characteristic of the past. Good schools, he argued, are necessary to "direct the child's activities, giv[e] them exercise along certain lines," and produce the "discipline, culture, and information" required for intellectual, moral, and social development.[27] To do so, good modern schools were necessary, but the existing American schools were not good modern schools. Dominated almost entirely by the medieval conception of learning, they were traditional schools, and they reflected their intellectual origins in Plato's theory of education for a "good" aristocratic social order.

As Dewey viewed existing American schools, they were dominated by the philosophy and methods of the "Old Education" and were stultifying places. For various reasons and in various ways, they were structured to suppress children's natural curiosity, eagerness to learn, and dynamic activism. Summarizing his indictment, Dewey charged that the typical points of the "Old Education" are "its passivity of attitude, its mechanical massing of children, its uniformity of curriculum and method. It may be summed up by stating that the center of gravity is outside the child. It is in the teacher, the textbook, anywhere and everywhere you please except in the immediate instinct and activities of the child himself."[28] In short, Dewey charged that the existing traditional American schools were unnatural institutions that confined, repressed, and failed children rather than directing and educating them healthily and liberally.

Designed to produce passive rather than active learners, schools were unwittingly programmed to cause children to fail; and to do so in various ways—fail to learn what schools taught and, therefore, experience schooling as a daily exercise in learned helplessness; fail to develop their individual talents and abilities; fail to get a good education; fail to become active, responsible, genuinely participatory members of social groups and communities. To replace traditional schools based on the "Old Education," which confined, repressed, and failed children, Dewey advocated a radically "New Education."

As Dewey theoretically conceived the "New Education," it would combine the best qualities of the preindustrial, informal natural learning system with the stimulating, liberating, and enlightening qualities of formal public schools organized according to the new "functional psychology" and "instrumentalist theory of knowledge" that he was developing. To test and develop his theoretical ideas, he organized the Laboratory School of the University of Chicago. Unfortunately, the scientistic strain in Dewey's thought led him to develop an "experimental" school, which, in practice, basically distorted the essence of his brilliant analysis of the benefits children gained from the real-world problem-solving foundation of the informal, natural learning system of preindustrial society. On balance, we contend, Dewey's Laboratory School worked against, rather than for, late-nineteenth- and twentieth-century efforts to reform the American public school system, "dominated almost entirely by the medieval conception of learning."[29]

Despite Dewey's brilliant insights and best intentions, the world-wide attention given to his Laboratory School tended to lead school reformers into a pedagogical blind alley. More precisely, its great theoretical "success" weakened the "community school movements" that episodically emerged during the twentieth century under a variety of names (e.g., social center, community center) and emphases. In direct contrast to the Laboratory School, community schools explicitly based themselves on the real-world household and community problem-solving orientation of the preindustrial learning system. In theory, as is evident in *The School and Society*, Dewey praised that orientation highly; in practice, his Laboratory School contradicted it fundamentally. To help explain the contradiction, it is critical to recognize that the operations of the Laboratory School were powerfully influenced by the experimental psychological laboratory Wilhelm Wundt had established in Germany and by Wundt's philosophical and psychological theories.

Wilhelm Wundt's Psychological Laboratory and Dewey's Scientistic Laboratory School

As is well known, Wilhelm Wundt of the University of Leipzig founded psychology as a separate discipline, and in 1879 created the first laboratory in the world dedicated to experimental psychology. As was not well known until recently, Wundt's theories and methodology powerfully influenced the development of Dewey's "functional psychology and instrumentalist version of psychology."[30] Once we recognize the powerful influence Wundt and his world-famous laboratory had on Dewey, we can see more clearly that Dewey's Laboratory School was quite literally conceived as a scientific laboratory to test and develop educational theories. And once we see that, we can better appreciate why the students in Dewey's Laboratory School could not benefit from the real-world problem solving that Dewey brilliantly theorized was the best way to engage their intense, sustained interest and develop their capacity for reflective critical inquiry and collaborative practical action. Critically examined, the Laboratory

School exemplified *scientism*, not science.[31] That is, we contend, Dewey used "un-Deweyan" means to try to achieve his instrumentalist, democratic, humanist goals for American public schools. Paradoxically, overcoming the anti-instrumentalist legacy of Dewey's Laboratory School is one of the main challenges contemporary school reformers have to meet to help achieve Dewey's instrumentalist educational goals.

Basically, the Laboratory School curriculum was sequentially organized around the history of American economic development. Proceeding from the early grades, children recapitulated in school aspects of the history of occupations that Americans had practiced in community and society from colonial days to the present. That is, consonant with Dewey's commitment to active rather than passive learning, as children advanced from grade to grade, they not only studied but "actually practiced" (in a very limited way, of course) the main occupations characteristic of successive generations of Americans.

Radically opposed to the "child listening" and "teacher talk"—to use a current term—orientation of traditional schools, the Laboratory School was *theoretically* organized around children working at practical occupations. The purpose, Dewey emphasized, was not "manual training" or "vocational training," it was to enable children attending formal schools to benefit from the functional equivalent of the active roles children played in the household and community life of preindustrial society. In the passage quoted below, Dewey summarizes the theory of formal education that guided his Laboratory School:

> Out of the occupation, out of doing things that are to produce results, and out of doing these in a social and cooperative way, there is born a discipline of its own kind and type. Our whole conception of school discipline changes when we get this point of view. In critical moments we all realize that the only training that becomes intuition, is that got through life itself. *That we learn from experience, and from books or the saying of others only as they are related to experience, are not mere phrases* [original emphasis]. . . . The great thing to keep in mind, then, regarding the introduction into the

school of various forms of active occupation, is that through them the entire spirit of the school is renewed. It has a chance to affiliate itself with life, to become the child's habitat, where he learns through directed living, instead of being only a place to learn lessons having an abstract and remote reference to some possible living to be done in the future. It gets a chance to be a miniature community, and embryonic society. This is the fundamental fact, and from this arise continuous and orderly streams of instruction.[32]

For our purposes, we need not present a detailed critique of Dewey's program to radically transform American public schools. We need only note that his Laboratory School did not—and by its scientistic, decontextualized nature could not—solve the problems he posed, namely, how to help children learn by "do[ing] things with a real motive behind and a real outcome ahead"[33]; how to connect effectively what children did in school with what they did outside of school; how to combine effectively the benefits of the preindustrial learning system with the benefits that could be derived from a modern, cosmopolitan, activity-based, formal schooling system; and how to minimize each system's particular disadvantages and optimize its advantages.

The Laboratory School of the University of Chicago was just that, an unnatural, artificial *university laboratory* isolated from American life as it really was lived or really had been lived. Rather than functioning as a natural laboratory that experimentally studied the real, complex links between school and community, the Laboratory School was effectively isolated from the community and society in which its pupils lived. In direct contrast, the informal learning system of preindustrial society was deeply rooted in, and functioned as an integral part of, the local geographic community in which children lived and their families made their livings.

Unlike the real occupations that children worked at in preindustrial communities from which they gained first-hand, direct experience of the real world, unlike the real problems they were forced to try to solve "with a real motive behind and a real outcome ahead," the occupations students practiced in the Laboratory School were make-believe, simulated occupations; moreover, the problems they solved were make-believe, simulated problems unconnected to real contemporary household or community problems. As Dewey acutely and strongly emphasized, in the preindustrial informal learning system, children learned by real-world, consequential doing. But in the isolated, artificial Laboratory School, which his scientism led him to develop, children learned by simulated, make-believe, inconsequential doing of well-structured problems whose solutions were well-known, presented no real challenge, and required no real imagination or initiative. The Laboratory School was—and could only be—a simulated pseudo-community, not a real "miniature community" or" embryonic society." It did not practically connect school and community; it created a radical disjunction between them.

Given its scientistic nature, unusually great resources, extraordinarily high teacher-to-student ratio, and insulation from the intense conflicts fragmenting the American societal and schooling systems at the time, the laboratory school was remarkably unrepresentative of American public schools as they were, or as they possibly could be in the foreseeable future. Little to no reason existed, therefore, to believe that lessons learned from the Laboratory School could be transferred to traditional public schools and "ordinary" teachers without a great deal of highly sophisticated, painstaking analysis, translation, and adaptation. Even if the Laboratory School worked well for its own students, there was little reason to think that the model it developed could have worked well for the great majority of students in American public schools.[34]

As Robert Westbrook has observed, most Laboratory School "students were from professional families, many of them the children of Dewey's colleagues." To practice "Deweyan pedagogy" effectively in the simulated world of the laboratory school, teachers had "to be highly skilled professionals, thoroughly knowledgeable in the subject matter they were teaching, trained in child psychology, and skilled in the techniques of providing the stimulus necessary to make the subject matter part of the child's growing experience."[35] That the world-famous Laboratory School of the University of Chicago, directed by the world-famous Dewey, could attract those "highly skilled professionals" did not mean that traditional public schools would be able to do that.

Among other reasons, Dewey's crusade to transform the American public school failed because his scientism so distorted his practice that the *specific solution* he proposed was remarkably scholastic, academic, impractical, and unrealistic. We underscore "specific solution" because we strongly agree with his *general* theories, propositions, and orientation. Appropriately applied, we are convinced, Dewey's general ideas can be highly practical. They can radically transform contemporary American public schools for the better and, in the process, help solve the Dewey Problem—that is, help develop the means necessary to construct a participatory democratic American society.

Jane Addams, Hull House, and Dewey's Prophetic Essay "The School as Social Centre"

As emphasized above, William Rainey Harper powerfully influenced Dewey's work on education during his ten years at the University of Chicago. In some ways, however, Dewey benefited even more significantly from his warm friendship and close association with Jane Addams and the other Hull House settlement workers struggling to improve the quality of life for the immigrant residents of the poverty-stricken Chicago neighborhood in which Hull House was located. Their work—and the powerful theories they derived from it—led Dewey to see both the critical role that local communities played in American society and that public schools could function as the strategic agents to develop participatory democratic communities, which, in turn, could function as the organizational foundation of the "organic" participatory democratic society he had theoretically envisioned in his 1888 Democratic Manifesto.[36]

Jane Addams in Chicago and Lilliam Wald in New York City, as well as other deeply motivated, socially concerned, brilliantly creative settlement house workers, pioneered the transfer of social, health, cultural, and recreational services to the public schools of major U.S. cities at the turn of the twentieth century. Theoretically guided, community-based, community-engaged, feminist settlement leaders observed that though there were very few settlement houses, there were very many public schools. Inspired by their innovative ideas and impressed by their practical community activities, in 1902 Dewey presented a brilliantly prophetic, highly influential address, "The School as Social Centre," at a National Educational Association conference.[37]

Viewed in historical perspective, Dewey's address clearly anticipated some of the key ideas and principles of the variously named "community school" movements that episodically rose and fell in the United States during the twentieth century and are rising again now. Thanks in very considerable measure to his close association with Jane Addams and Hull House, by 1902 Dewey experienced Chicago differently than he had in 1894 when he first conceived and began to organize what became the laboratory school. That may explain why the concrete, practical content of his address to the National Educational Association differed so radically from the abstract philosophical and theoretical concerns that had motivated him to organize the Laboratory School. At any rate, the opening paragraph of his address indicates this dramatic shift in his thinking.

> According to the character of my invitation to speak to you, I shall confine myself to the philosophy of the school as a social centre. I accept the invitation with pleasure, but at the same time I do not feel that the philosophical aspect of the matter is the urgent or important one. *The pressing thing, the significant thing, is really to make the school a social centre; that is a matter of practice, not of theory* [emphasis added]. Just what to do in order to make the schoolhouse a centre of full and adequate social service to bring it completely into the current of social life, such are the matters, I am sure, which really deserve the attention of the public and that occupy your own minds.[38]

Having explicitly set aside abstract philosophical questions to focus on practical questions, Dewey then located the "social centre" idea in its historical context: "What forces are stirring that awaken such speedy and favorable response to the notion that the school, as a place of instruction for children, is not performing its full function—that it needs also to operate as a centre of life for all ages and classes?" To answer that question, Dewey briefly sketched the history of education from "the schools carried on by great philosophical organizations of antiquity—the Platonic, Stoic, Epicurean, etc.," to the medieval schools "as a phase of the work of the church," to the "modern types of public, or at least quasi-public school."[39]

When the State took control of education, Dewey observed, it inevitably restricted "the school . . . exclusively . . . [to] one function, the purveying of intellectual material to a number of selected minds." Even when the "democratic impulse broke" into the functioning of the school, it did "not effect a complete reconstruction" but only added the limited element of

> preparation for citizenship. The meaning of this phrase, "preparation for citizenship," shows precisely what I have in mind by the difference between the school as an isolated thing related to the state alone, and the school as a thoroughly socialized affair in contact at all points with the flow of community life. . . . Now our community life has suddenly awakened; and in awakening it has found that governmental institutions and affairs represent only a small part of the important purposes and difficult problems of life, and that even that fraction cannot be dealt with adequately except in the light of a wide range of domestic, economic, and scientific considerations excluded from the conception of the state of citizenship.[40]

Moreover, the concept of citizenship itself was expanding greatly, Dewey observed. As "industrial and commercial changes and adjustments"[41] produced a much more interactive, complex society, the isolation between state and society, between the government and the institutions of family, business life, etc. is breaking down. . . . *The content of the term "citizenship" is broadening; it is coming to mean all the relationships of all sorts that are involved in membership in a community* [emphasis added].

That is why the "existing type of education . . . [is] defective."

Change the image of what constitutes citizenship and you change the image of what is the purpose of the school. Change this, and you change the picture of what the school should be doing and of how it should be doing it. The feeling that the school is not doing all that it should do in simply giving instruction during the day to a certain number of children of different ages, the demand that it shall assume a wider scope of activities having an educative effect upon the adult members of the community has its basis just here: We are feeling everywhere the organic unity of the different modes of social life, and consequently demand that the school shall be related more widely, shall receive from more quarters, and shall give in more directions.[42]

Pointing out the growing disparity of "simply giving instruction to a certain number of children" and the broader role required of schooling, Dewey then briefly discussed the restricted nature of the "older idea of the school" and why the rapid increase in societal complexity resulted in our having "lost a good deal of our faith in the efficacy of purely intellectual instruction."[43] To account for that loss of faith and to justify the innovative use of the "School as Social Centre," Dewey analyzed four developments.

1. "The much-increased efficiency and ease of all the agencies that have to do with bringing people into contact with one another," which resulted from technological and organizational innovations in transportation and communication.

2. "A relaxation of social discipline and control," which meant that schools would have to take on new responsibilities and methods for the moral education of both children and adults.

3. An unprecedented expansion of knowledge and "intellectual life" into "all other affairs of life," which made a "purely and exclusively intellectual instruction" less meaningful than in any previous era.

4. The "demand and opportunity" for the "prolongation, under modern conditions, of continuous instruction."[44]

Dewey's observations about the fourth development accounting for the rapidly growing strength of the "school as social centre" movement are particularly insightful, prescient, and relevant for contemporary society. Dewey emphasized that the need for "continuous instruction"—"lifelong learning" as we now call it—was no longer restricted to the "learned professions"; it had become nearly universal.

> Now, what is true of the lawyer and the doctor, in the more progressive sections of the country, is true to a certain extent of all sorts and degrees of people. Social, economic and intellectual conditions are changing at a rate undreamed of in past history. Now, unless the agencies of instruction are kept running more or less parallel with these changes, a considerable body of men [i.e., people] is bound to find itself without the training which will enable it to adapt itself to what is going on. It will be left stranded and become a burden for the community to carry. *Where progress is continuous and certain, education must be equally certain and continuous* [emphasis added].[45]

Having "hastily sketched" the "fourfold need and . . . fourfold opportunity" that "defines to some extent the work of the school as a social centre," Dewey then summarized his prescription for what it must do.

> It must provide at least part of that training which is necessary to keep the individual properly adjusted to a rapidly

changing environment. It must interpret to him the intellectual and social meaning of the work in which he is engaged: that is, must reveal its relations to the life and work of the world. It must make up to him in part for the decay of dogmatic and fixed methods of social discipline. It must supply him compensation for the loss of reverence and the influence of authority. And, finally, it must provide means for bringing people and their ideas and beliefs together, in such ways as will lessen friction and instability, and introduce deeper sympathy and wider understanding.[46]

Dewey then posed the critical question: how could the school as social center perform the multiple tasks that he assigned it? Though disavowing any attempt to try to answer the question in detail, he thought it appropriate to "indicate certain general lines."[47]

As the quotation below strongly suggests, Dewey's ideas about the school as a social center were directly and deeply shaped by his work with Jane Addams and others at Hull House. The quotation also supports our general proposition that the neighborhood orientation and "heroic" work of settlement house staff members directly inspired and shaped the "school-based social center" and "community center" movements of the twentieth century. "Every neighborhood public school a neighborhood settlement house," can be said to be the vision impelling settlement leaders to function as strategically important school reformers during the late-nineteenth and twentieth centuries. Dewey explicitly applauded their vision in his answer to the question of how the school as a social center could perform the various "tasks" he assigned it. The following makes that very clear:

First, there is mixing people up with each other: bringing them together under wholesome influences and under conditions which will promote their getting acquainted with the best side of each other. I suppose, whenever we are framing our ideals of the school as a social centre, what we think of is particularly the better class of social settlements. *What we want is to see the school, every public school, doing something of the same sort of work that is now done by a settlement or two scattered at wide distances through the city* [emphasis added]. And we all know that the work of such an institution as Hull House has been primarily not that of conveying intellectual instruction, but of being a social clearinghouse.

The function of the school as a social centre in promoting social meetings for social purposes suggests at once another function—provision and direction of reasonable forms of amusement and recreation. The social club, the gymnasium, the amateur theatrical representation, the concert, the stereopticon lecture—these are agencies the force of which social settlements have long known, and which are coming into use whenever anything is doing in the way of making schools social centres.

In the third place, there ought to be some provision for a sort of continuous social selection of a somewhat "specialized" type—using "specialized," of course, in a relative sense. . . . *To refer once more to the working model upon which I am pretty continuously drawing, in the activities of Hull House we find provision made for classes in music, drawing, clay-modelling, joinery, metal-working, and so on* [emphasis added]. There is no reason why something by way of scientific laboratories should not be provided for those who are particularly interested in problems of mechanics or electricity; and so the list might be continued.[48]

Dewey concludes his address by emphasizing the unique role that the school could play in the development of community life and in realizing the potential of "the community" to raise human society to a higher level of development.

In conclusion, we may say that the conception of the school as a social centre is born of our entire democratic movement. Everywhere we see signs of the growing recognition that the community owes to each one of its members the fullest opportunity for development. Everywhere we see the growing recognition that the community life is defective and distorted excepting as it thus does care for all its constituent parts. This is no longer viewed as a matter of charity, but as a matter of justice—nay, even of something higher and better than justice—a necessary phase of developing and growing life. Men [i.e., people] will long dispute about material socialism, about socialism considered as a matter of distribution of the material resources of the community: but this is a socialism about which there can be no such dispute—socialism of the intelligence and of the spirit. To extend the range and the fullness of sharing in the intellectual and spiritual resources of the community is the very meaning of the community. *Because the older type of education is not fully adequate to this task under changed conditions, we feel its lack and demand that the school shall become a social centre* [emphasis added].[49]

The Schooling System as the Strategic Subsystem of Modern Societies

Having paid Dewey the homage of criticizing him harshly when we thought it appropriate, we now praise him highly for the strategic contributions "The School as Social Centre" made to the better analysis of the internal functioning of modern societal systems and, in particular, to the community school movements of the twentieth century. Perhaps Dewey's greatest contribution was his farsighted observation that, during the twentieth century, the schooling system would function as the strategic subsystem of the increasingly complex industrial and "postindustrial" societies produced by the post-1800 economic and communication revolutions. To use the term now in vogue, Dewey predicted that the school-based operations of "civil society" would become more important than the traditional functions performed by the State in solving "the difficult problems of life." Just as Dewey saw citizenship expanding to take on functions that were beyond the capacity of the State in an advanced capitalist society, he saw an expanded role for the school in preparing citizens to assume these functions.

Extending Dewey's observations, particularly in the twenty-first century, it is not the judicial, legislative, and administrative State, but rather the complex schooling system of American society—from early childhood centers to elite research universities—that (1) must function as the *strategic subsystem* of the society; (2) has performed that function poorly—in the past and present—*at all levels*; (3) must radically improve its performance, at all levels, if we hope to solve the problems of American life in the twenty-first century; and (4) can only be radically reformed if questions about its performance—in the past, present, and likely future—are given the highest priority by action-oriented researchers and administrators dedicated to advancing knowledge for "the relief of man's estate,"[50] which Francis Bacon long ago specified as the goal of science.

No implication is intended, of course, that in 1902 Dewey said exactly what we have just stated. Because we stand on his shoulders and are blessed by 20/20 hindsight, however, we believe that the course of history justifies our far-reaching extension of what he actually did say in 1902. We prefigure our later argument here to suggest why we regard "The School as Social Centre" so highly, as well as how much it has influenced our "neo-Deweyan" strategy to achieve a participatory democratic schooling system and participatory democratic American society. What the *Communist Manifesto* was for Karl Marx, it seems not too far-fetched to suggest, "The School as Social Centre" was for John Dewey.

As we have tried to show, the increasing need for "lifelong learning" was one main reason Dewey assigned the school such a highly strategic role in modern society. Present-day manifestos about the great importance of "lifelong learning" represent little more than a gloss on Dewey's farsighted proposition in 1902 that "the community" had the responsibility of providing, "through the school as a centre, a continuous education for all classes of whatever age"[51]—a proposition that significantly influenced what we generically term the "community-school movement" (e.g., "school as social center," as "community center") of the twentieth century.

Rather than list all of Dewey's brilliant propositions and predictions, we conclude our analysis of the contributions he made in "The

School as Social Centre" by discussing his claim that, properly conceived and organized and conducted, the school has a unique—and uniquely important—capacity: By its very nature, it could produce unlimited Goods of the type necessary for full personal development of all members of the community. These Goods are "the intangible things of art, science, and other modes of social intercourse," and these Goods are not finite. Because they are unlimited Goods, to secure them, neither individuals nor communities need to compete in zero-sum games. On the contrary, "social intercourse" focused on the production of such Goods could both enrich and strengthen the community to the extent that its members collaboratively engaged in such intercourse. That is what Dewey meant to connote by his reference to the "socialism of the intelligence and of the spirit."[52]

For the school to help produce that Deweyan kind of "socialism," however, it must greatly enlarge its role and must function as the social center of the community. Put another way, by 1902 Dewey viewed the school as uniquely well positioned to function as the central institution of the local community because—in principle, though not yet in practice—it was uniquely well positioned to bring about a socialism of Goods relating to "the intelligence" and "the spirit." Much of the history of the twentieth century community school movements can be summarized as a series of failed attempts to find and develop the concrete practices needed to realize in fact what Dewey believed community schools could do in abstract principle.

Having praised Dewey for his strategic contributions in "The School as Social Centre," we think it is important to recognize that he then had little or nothing to say about two critically important functions the community school might perform: 1) the school as a community institution actively engaged in the solution of community problems; and 2) the school as a community institution that educated children, both intellectually and morally, by engaging them *appropriately* and *significantly* in real-world community problem-solving—as children had been educated in the informal natural learning system of preindustrial society. Dewey ignored those two possible community school functions, even though they were logically entailed by his general theory of "learning by doing."

At the risk of sounding hyperbolic, we restate our admiration for Dewey's farsighted, creative analysis of the complex consequences of the "industrial and commercial changes and adjustments"[53] that produced a radically new type of society in the late-nineteenth and twentieth centuries. Dewey did not use the specific terms, "advanced industrial society" and "world economy," but those terms designate some of the phenomena emphasized in his analysis. Somewhat freely interpreted, Dewey argued that the development of advanced industrial societies in an increasingly worldwide economy produced an unprecedented set of complex societal problems—so unprecedented and so complex as to require radical reconstruction of social and political theory.

Existing social and political theories could not provide good solutions for the multitude of problems that suddenly were manifesting themselves in advanced industrial societies. They could not do so because they had been inspired by very different types of problems in very different types of societies. Dewey claimed that neither the operations of the private enterprise "free-market" system developed in the nineteenth century nor the operation of the governmental systems as they had traditionally functioned over the centuries could solve the new and myriad problems produced by the new type of advanced industrial society. As we read "The School as Social Centre," it represents a pioneering, highly insightful attempt to reconstruct and update social and economic theory to deal more effectively with the unprecedented set of problems confronting members of advanced industrial societies in the twentieth century.

If neither the operations of the "free-market" nor the traditional operations of government could cope with the complex societal problems of the twentieth century, which institution—or combination of institutions—could? Dewey's answer to the questions he posed essentially pointed to the local community. To repeat a previous quotation:

> Everywhere we see signs of the growing recognition that the community owes to each one of its members the fullest opportunity for development. Everywhere we see the growing recognition that the community life is defective and distorted

excepting as it thus does care for all its constituents. This is no longer viewed as a matter of charity, but as a matter of justice—nay, even of something higher and better than justice—a necessary phase of developing and growing life.[54]

How specifically could the community carry out those unprecedented responsibilities? Primarily, Dewey answered, *through the neighborhood school* organized and functioning as a social center "for all classes of whatever ages."[55] In essence, inspired by the work of Jane Addams's Hull House, Dewey's pioneering reconstruction of social and political theory called for the neighborhood school to function as a publicly owned site, a publicly controlled and organized catalyst, to bring people together and to develop local coalitions of neighbors to solve the multitude of problems suddenly emerging in advanced industrial societies.

As noted previously, viewed in historical perspective, Dewey's 1902 address clearly anticipated some of the key ideas of the democratic "community school movements" that episodically rose and fell in the United States during the twentieth century. As will be explored later in this book, his ideas about communities and community schools can be logically extended and developed to help provide a practical solution to what has been previously identified as the Dewey Problem. Terribly oversimplified here for brevity's sake, our proposed solution takes this form: Appropriately developed and powerfully assisted by higher education institutions and other community organizations, community schools can help create cohesive "organic communities" that enable all community members to participate "in the formation of the common will," feel that they are full members of a "commonwealth," and really have a "share in society."

Unfortunately for the development of participatory democracy, that possible "solution" to the Dewey Problem only represents our own logical extension and development of the powerful ideas Dewey prophetically sketched in "The School as Social Centre." Unfortunately, after 1902 he himself did almost nothing to extend and develop his ideas along those lines.

3   Dewey Leaves the University of Chicago for Columbia University

In its deepest and richest sense a community must always remain a matter of face-to-face intercourse. . . . There is no substitute for the vitality and depth of close and direct intercourse and attachment. . . . Democracy must begin at home, and its home is the neighborly community.

JOHN DEWEY, THE PUBLIC AND ITS PROBLEMS (1927)

SOON AFTER HIS 1902 ADDRESS to the National Education Association, John Dewey quarreled with William Rainey Harper and others over the operation of the remarkably comprehensive School of Education, which Harper had finally succeeded in creating to implement his long-held vision of a highly integrated schooling system, from kindergarten through university. As a result of those quarrels, Dewey decided to trade his position at a university that was directly and actively engaged in the problems of its city for one in the traditionally scholastic Department of Philosophy at Columbia University.[1]

In light of Dewey's vision of the transforming role schools could play as social centers, his departure from Chicago in 1904 was a tragic mistake, which had devastating consequences for the American schooling system—and American society—in the twentieth century. It was a tragic mistake because, among other reasons, Harper had created an unprecedentedly comprehensive university school of education in 1902 and had appointed Dewey its director. It seems reasonable to conjecture the following: given the "engaged" culture and environment of Chicago and the powerful assistance of Harper, the School of Education, and the innovative, community-engaged Department of Philosophy and Psychology (which Dewey had built and continued to chair after his appointment as director), Dewey could eventually have mobilized the resources needed to put into practice his "radical" vision of neighborhood public schools as social centers. Instead of following that strategic course of action, however, he allowed himself to become bitterly embroiled in bureaucratic battles for personal control of the School of Education. As a result, he departed for Columbia, presided over by the elitist Nicholas Murray Butler, and the Harper-Dewey vision of a highly integrated, democratic, American schooling system lost any chance it might have had to be realized.

After leaving Chicago and joining the Department of Philosophy at Columbia, Dewey essentially concentrated on the professional reconstruction of the academic discipline of philosophy and made little effort to practically connect universities with elementary and secondary schools. For example, despite the powerful theory advanced in "The School as Social Centre," he never tried to develop and implement it. By using the extraordinary resources at Columbia's Teachers College, he could have mobilized them to help shape democratic community schools in New York City and thereby helped to develop education as a discipline in concrete real-world practice rather than abstract, contemplative, academic theory. Instead, he increasingly worked to bring about *Reconstruction in Philosophy*, the title of the major book he published in 1920. As that title suggests, after moving to New York, Dewey came to believe that reconstructing the traditional discipline of philosophy, not reconstructing the traditional schooling system, was the best strategy to advance democracy and the betterment of humanity.

Dewey Abandons Any Attempt to Integrate Schooling Theory and Schooling Practice

After he left Chicago, of course, Dewey published many works more or less relevant to education. But he essentially abandoned any attempt to *develop schooling theory by testing and integrating it with schooling practice.* The following is Westbrook's characteristically perceptive assessment of the severely adverse consequences:

> Although Dewey landed on his feet at Columbia, his losses were considerable. He gave up leadership of the collaborative "real school" of philosophy William James had celebrated, and he abandoned the elementary school that was the only practical expression of his philosophy of education. This latter loss seems to me particularly important, for it not only left it to others to interpret, apply and usually distort Dewey's pedagogical ideas but also deprived him of the one concrete manifestation of his democratic ideals that he could point to and say, *"This* is what I have in mind."[2]

In 1947, Harold Rugg, a leading authority on American education and a colleague of Dewey's at Columbia, bitterly pointed out the larger adverse consequences for school and society of what he characterized as "Mr. Dewey's Withdrawal from Educational Reconstruction."

> Mr. Dewey left Chicago in the summer of 1904 to become Professor of Philosophy at Columbia University. During the next decade his influence was at a low ebb. I am told by those who knew him well at that time that he regarded his work in educational reconstruction of little avail, and for over forty years he has refrained from practical experimentation in schools.
>
> These negative facts of Mr. Dewey's virtual and, I think, discouraged, withdrawal from the active building of sound schools are in my judgment very important. If he had continued in *educational reconstruction*, instead of turning to "reconstruction in philosophy," as he did, I am confident that many of the worst mistakes made by the so-called "progressive" schools would not have been made. But he did withdraw, never to return throughout forty years of vigorous and creative work.[3]

As the quotation from Rugg suggests, after Dewey left Chicago he increasingly lost faith in the schooling system as the strategic agency to help democratize the American societal system. Dewey's loss of faith clearly manifested itself in one of his most famous books, *Democracy and Education*. Published in 1916, it emphasized the highly important role of "education" in a democratic society.[4] But it explicitly asserted that, "compared with other agencies," *schools* only function as a "relatively superficial means"[5] of what Dewey now meant by the extraordinarily inclusive term "education." In a sense, in *Democracy and Education*, Dewey reverted to the theory of *communication and society* that had led him to participate so enthusiastically in the *Thought News* enterprise with Franklin Ford in Michigan.

The title of the introductory chapter of *Democracy and Education* is "Education as a Necessity of Life." Like all other living beings, Dewey noted, human beings renew their species by a process of "transmission." Human society, he wrote,

> exists through a process of transmission quite as much as biological life. This transmission occurs by means of communication of habits of doing, thinking, and feeling from the older to the younger. Without this communication of ideals, hopes, expectations, standards, opinions, from those members of society who are passing out of the group life to those who are coming into it, social life could not survive. . . . Yet this renewal is not automatic. Unless pains are taken to see that genuine and thorough transmission takes place, the most civilized group will relapse into barbarism and then into savagery.[6]

Why dwell on the truism that teaching and learning are necessary for a society to continue to exist? Dewey's answer was that

> justification is found in the fact that such emphasis is a means of getting us away from an unduly scholastic and formal notion of education. Schools are, indeed, one important method of the transmission which forms the dispositions of the immature; but it is only one means, and, compared with

other agencies, a relatively superficial means. Only as we have grasped the necessity of more fundamental and persistent modes of tuition can we make sure of placing the scholastic methods in their true context.[7]

Having placed schools in their true context, Dewey argued, we can see that *communication* is the strategic agency of "education" and "community":

> Society not only continues to exist *by* transmission, *by* communication, but it may fairly be said to exist *in* transmission, *in* communication [original emphasis]. There is more than a verbal tie between the words common, community, and communication. Men [i.e., people] live in a community in virtue of the things they have in common; *and communication is the way in which they come to possess things in common* [emphasis added]. What they must have in common in order to form a community or society are aims, beliefs, aspirations, knowledge—a common understanding—like-mindedness as the sociologists say. . . . Persons do not become a society by living in physical proximity, any more than a man ceases to be socially influenced by being so many feet or miles removed from others. A book or a letter may institute a more intimate association between human beings separated thousands of miles from each other than exists between dwellers under the same roof. . . . Not only is social life identical with communication, but all communication (and hence all genuine social life) is educative. . . . All communication is like art. It may fairly be said, therefore, that any social arrangement that remains vitally social, or vitally shared, is educative to those who participate in it.[8]

For the young, of course, formal education is vitally important as civilization advances because "learning by direct sharing in the pursuits of grown-ups becomes increasingly difficult":

But there are conspicuous dangers attendant upon the transition from indirect to formal education. Sharing in actual pursuits, whether directly or vicariously in play, is at least personal and vital. These qualities compensate in some measure, for the narrowness of available opportunities. Formal instruction, on the contrary, easily becomes remote and dead—abstract and bookish, to use the ordinary words of depreciation. . . . As societies become more complex in structure and resources, the need of formal or intentional teaching and learning increases. [But as] . . . formal teaching and training grow in extent, there is the danger of creating an undesirable split between the experience gained in more direct associations and what is acquired in school. This danger was never greater than at the present time, on account of the rapid growth in the last few centuries of knowledge and technical modes of skill.[9]

We risk belaboring the obvious, but it is clear that the Dewey of *Democracy and Education*, which was written at Columbia, was radically different than the Dewey of "The School as Social Centre," which was written at Chicago. Not only did he now deprecate schools as a "relatively superficial means" of education for children and adults in a democratic society, *he now also sharply deprecated the role of local geographical communities*. Because communication across space could produce far more "intimate association between human beings" than could be produced by their living in "physical proximity," he now asserted that cohesive, vital communities could consist of human beings "separated thousands of miles from each other."

After publishing *Democracy and Education* in 1916, Dewey continued to pay relatively little attention to schools as agencies of democracy and education. But by 1927, he had, to an astonishing extent, radically reversed his 1916 position on the role played by local geographical communities in a democratic society, a reversal that he never explained. To an even greater extent than in his 1902 "School as Social Centre" address, he now emphasized the strategic role local communities played as "agencies" of democracy. In fact, he now viewed the face-to-face "neighborly community" as the vital "home" of democracy, its most important agency.

Dewey vs. Lippmann: Participatory Democracy and Face-to-Face Neighborly Communities

Dewey published *The Public and Its Problems* in 1927 to counteract antidemocratic ideas and movements gaining strength in the United States and elsewhere during the 1920s. It constituted his major work on politics. A leading Dewey specialist hails it as "the culmination of Dewey's instrumentalism."[10]

As we read *The Public and Its Problems*, the book exemplifies and illuminates Dewey's conception of the primary societal role of "the American Scholar." The function of American Scholars is to act as engaged "Public Intellectuals," not as solipsistic scholastics engaged in intramural battles for power, prestige, and cash within an Ivory Tower. To support our assessment, we briefly sketch the contemporary political and social conflicts that inspired Dewey to once again proclaim the Democratic Manifesto he had first proclaimed in 1888.

The horrors of World War I and the corrosive disillusionment that resulted after 1918 undermined optimism and strengthened pessimism. Compared to the pre-1914 era of hope and enthusiasm, the intellectual and political climates of opinion in Western societies changed remarkably. Caustically attacked as naively unrealistic and societally dysfunctional, once dominant progressive social and political theories lost much of their power to influence opinion, policy, and action. As a result, prewar radicals, such as Walter Lippmann, abandoned progressivism to assert a set of "realistic" claims about modern society, distilled as follows:

After 1800, material abundance increased greatly as a result of industrialism and scientific and technological advances. Those "forces" also created interdependent national societies characterized by massive urbanization and an ever-expanding large-scale State. But the new type of society that evolved during the late-nineteenth and early twentieth centuries—the "Great Society" as Graham Wallas ironically dubbed it in 1914—functioned as an increasingly atomistic, alienated society. That is, given the nature of the forces and processes that produced it, the "Great Society" essentially functioned as a "mass society" with highly dangerous characteristics (e.g., bewildering complexity, atomism, alienation, apathy, ignorance, excitability, sensation seeking, and cynical manipulation of gullible enfranchised masses vulnerable to demagogy and propaganda).

Suppose we grant the validity of the "industrial society equals mass society" formula. It follows, then, that ideas of popular democracy constituted dangerous delusions. Self-labeled "realists" such as Walter Lippmann and Joseph Schumpeter argued in this vein that democratic theory must be reconstructed along the lines of what later came to be known as "elitist democracy." Elitist democratic theories call for political and social systems that allow the mass of citizens (or members) only very limited power to influence governmental (or institutional) decisions, namely, the power to vote and *choose between (or among) elites competing for office or authority.*

It was in that context that Dewey wrote *The Public and Its Problems.* Written to defend—and extend—democratic theory against Lippmann (and other critics), it argues passionately for participatory democracy. By 1927, of course, Dewey was far more professionally secure than he had been in 1888, when he had only briefly and vaguely observed that "democracy is not in reality what it is in name until it is industrial, as well as civil and political."[11] Accordingly, in *The Public and Its Problems* he spelled out much more clearly what participatory democracy entailed than he had felt secure enough to do in his 1888 essay on "Ethics of Democracy."

> We have had occasion to refer in passing to the distinction between democracy as a social idea and political democracy as a system of government. The two are, of course, connected. The idea remains barren and empty save as it is incarnated in human relationships. Yet in discussion they must be distinguished. The idea of democracy is a wider and fuller idea than can be exemplified in the state even at its best. To be realized it must affect all modes of human association, the

family, the school, industry, religion. . . . In a search for the conditions under which the inchoate public now extant may function democratically, we may proceed from a statement of the nature of the democratic idea in its generic social sense. *From the standpoint of the individual, it consists in having a responsible share according to capacity in forming and directing the activities of the groups to which one belongs and in participating according to need in the values which the groups sustain* [emphasis added]. From the standpoint of the groups, it demands liberation of potentialities of members of a group in harmony with the interests and goods which are common. . . . A good citizen finds his conduct as a member of a potential group enriching and enriched by his participation in family life, industry, scientific and artistic associations. There is a free give-and-take: fullness of integrated personality is therefore possible of achievement, since the pulls and responses of different groups reinforce one another and their values accord. Regarded as an idea, democracy is not an alternative to other principles of associated life. It is the idea of community life itself. . . . *The clear consciousness of a communal life, in all its implications, constitutes the idea of democracy* [emphasis added].[12]

Dewey now claimed that participatory democracy not only was highly desirable as an abstract theory of human equality, it was realistically possible under certain conditions. What were those conditions? For our purposes, we need only consider Dewey's primary condition: to be realized in practice, participatory democracy required the construction of "democratic, cosmopolitan, neighborly communities" (our term for Dewey's proposition). Such communities would function as the basic social units—the foundations—of advanced industrial societies. Given their nature, Dewey believed, they would prevent advanced industrial societies from becoming mass societies and would advance and make possible the development of participatory democracy.

Democratic Theory and the Construction of Democratic, Cosmopolitan, Neighborly Communities

According to Dewey, history had not discredited democratic theory; instead, it had discredited naive ideas of inevitable accelerating progress and expanding popular democracy. Ideas of that type were poorly founded and had serious defects. Among other things, their enthusiastic proponents had failed to recognize that the post-1800 economic and communication revolutions had great costs in addition to their benefits. The greatest cost was that they had powerfully undermined the foundations of the traditional local communities that had evolved over millennia. Reflecting a dominant tendency in European and American social theory, Dewey asserted that the disintegration of local communities had severely negative consequences for human well-being. If human societies are to function effectively, *they must be based on face-to-face local communities that function effectively.*

> In its deepest and richest sense a community must always remain a matter of face-to-face intercourse. This is why the family and neighborhood, with all their deficiencies, have always been the chief agencies of nurture, the means by which dispositions are stably formed and ideas acquired which laid hold on the roots of character. . . . The invasion and partial destruction of the life of the . . . [face-to-face local community] by outside uncontrolled agencies is the immediate source of the instability, disintegration and restlessness which characterize the present epoch. Evils which are uncritically and indiscriminately laid at the door of industrialism and democracy might, with greater intelligence, be referred to the dislocation and unsettlement of local communities. Vital and thorough attachments are bred only in the intimacy of an intercourse which is of necessity restricted in range. . . . *There is no substitute for the vitality and depth of close and direct intercourse and attachment.* . . . *Democracy must begin at home, and its home is the neighborly community* [emphasis added].[13]

As the quotation shows, Dewey directly contradicted social theorists who claimed that industrialism necessarily eroded the foundations of local communities and made mass society inevitable. To counter their arguments, he offered the optimistic possibility that local communities could be reconstructed in the future because they were vitally necessary for human well-being. Given their vital role in the organization of human societies, he contended, they might again become "genuine centers of the attention, interest and devotion for their constituent members."[14] Moreover, since Dewey—arguably the quintessential American optimist—still strongly believed in the likelihood of social progress, he further assumed that the reconstructed local communities of the future would be superior, in the most important aspects, to their preindustrial predecessors. This assumption is central to his argument—and ours:

> There is something deep within human nature itself which pulls toward settled relationships. Inertia and the tendency toward stability belong to emotions and desires as well as to masses and molecules. That happiness which is full of content and peace is found only in enduring ties with others, which reach to such depths that they go below the surface of conscious experience to form its undisturbed foundations. No one knows how much of the frothy excitement of life, of mania for motion, of fretful discontent, of need for artificial stimulation, is the expression of the frantic search for something to fill the void caused by the loosening of bonds which hold persons together in immediate community of experience.[15]

Radically contradicting the position he had taken a decade earlier in *Democracy and Education*, Dewey now theorized that local communities express and reflect "something deep within human nature itself" and maintained the hopeful prospect that the "new local community" (our term for his concept) of the future would transcend the traditional local community of the past.

Whatever the future may have in store, one thing is certain. Unless local communal life can be restored, the public cannot adequately resolve its most urgent problem: to find and identify itself. But if it be reestablished, *it will manifest a fullness, variety and freedom of possession and enjoyment of meanings and goods unknown in the contiguous associations of the past* [emphasis added]. For it will be alive and flexible as well as stable, responsive to the complex and world-wide scene in which it is enmeshed. While local, it will not be isolated. Its larger relationships will provide an inexhaustible and flowing fund of meanings upon which to draw, with assurance that its drafts will be honored. Territorial states and political boundaries will persist; but they will not be barriers which impoverish experience by cutting man off from his fellows; they will not be hard and fast divisions whereby external separation is converted into inner jealousy, fear, suspicion and hostility. Competition will continue, but it will be less rivalry for acquisition of material goods, and more an emulation of local groups to enrich direct experience with appreciatively enjoyed intellectual and artistic wealth. If the technological age can provide mankind with a firm and general basis of material security, it will be absorbed in a humane age. It will take its place as an instrumentality of shared and communicated experience.[16]

Dewey's theory asserts that the new type of local community could function as the basic social component of a worldwide "Great Community," which would progressively transcend the worldwide "Great Society" rapidly emerging in the twentieth century. To conclude the 1927 version of his Democratic Manifesto, therefore, he restated the uniquely important role his theory assigned to face-to-face interaction in the "generation of democratic communities and an articulate democratic public":[17]

The problem of securing diffused and seminal intelligence can be solved only in the degree in which local communal life becomes a reality. Signs and symbols, language, are the means of communication by which a fraternally shared experience is ushered in and sustained. *But the winged words of conversation in immediate intercourse have a vital import lacking in the fixed and frozen words of written speech* [emphasis added]. . . . There is no limit to the liberal expansion and confirmation of limited personal intellectual endowment which may proceed from the flow of social intelligence when that circulates by word of mouth from one to another in the communications of the local community. That and that only gives reality to public opinion. We lie, as Emerson said, in the lap of an immense intelligence. *But that intelligence is dormant and its communications are broken, inarticulate and faint until it possesses the local community as its medium* [emphasis added].[18]

Despite the widespread disillusionment after World War I, Dewey still optimistically believed that advancing science and technology could function as the precondition for a "humane age." Also, Dewey's optimism unequivocally rested on his assumption that human beings would find ways to construct a radically new type of local community—one that transcended the limitations and defects of the traditional local community.

As the quotations above show, Dewey still retained enough of his Hegelian organic philosophy to envision the new local community as a highly progressive, humanistic synthesis of old and new. It would constitute an unprecedented form of social organization—one which retained the desirable qualities of the traditional local community while dynamically combining them with the liberating and stimulating qualities made possible by the accelerating economic and communication revolutions. The new local community would be a democratic, cosmopolitan, neighborly community that remained rooted in a particular place, with particular qualities, relationships, loyalties, and history, while simultaneously embodying, expressing, and benefiting from universal humane values, qualities, and affiliations. As Dewey envisioned the new type of neighborly community, it would constitute the organizational foundation of the worldwide "Great Community," which had its origins in the Scientific Revolution of the seventeenth century and the great advances in science and technology after 1800.

It perhaps belabors a point to note that technological advances such as the Internet simultaneously connect traditional local communities to universal values and affiliations and contribute to weakening those communities. Regardless, Dewey's argument is that democratic, cosmopolitan, face-to-face, neighborly communities are *necessary* for a democratic society.

In our judgment, Dewey brilliantly and correctly identified the central problem that human societies now confront, namely, the problem of constructing democratic, cosmopolitan, neighborly communities in the age of the global economy, global communication systems, supranational corporations, and global terror.

Most importantly, however, is to emphasize this point: having brilliantly identified the central problem confronting human beings in the twentieth century, Dewey then resorted to sophistry to evade his responsibility to present a possible solution to it *or* rather to suggest an intelligent strategy to develop a solution to it. To justify that harsh assessment, we note that Dewey had explicitly stated that *The Public and Its Problems* was specifically designed to answer these basic questions:

> What are the conditions under which it is possible for the Great Society to approach more closely and vitally the status of a Great Community, and thus take form in genuinely democratic societies and states? What are the conditions under which we may reasonably picture the Public emerging from its eclipse?[19]

In the very next paragraph, however, Dewey explained to his readers that he would make no effort to answer those questions empirically and practically, no effort to suggest how or why, or even if, the necessary conditions might be realized:

The study will be an intellectual or hypothetical one. There will be no attempt to state how the required conditions might come into existence, nor to prophesy that they will occur. The object of the analysis will be to show that *unless* [original emphasis] ascertained specifications are realized, the Community cannot be organized as a democratically effective Public. It is not claimed that the conditions which will be noted will suffice, but only that at least they are indispensable.[20]

How can Dewey's evasive disclaimer be reasonably characterized other than sophistry? He had argued that the construction of democratic, cosmopolitan, neighborly communities was the "indispensable" condition for the transformation of "Great Societies" into the "Great Community" needed to organize "a democratically effective Public."[21] Antidemocratic "realists," however, were surely entitled to dismiss Dewey's indispensable condition as a truly impossible dream—an ideologically determined, dangerously utopian delusion—unless he suggested how that condition could be realized, how and why specific types of human agents could reasonably be expected to act in ways likely to bring it about, given the realities of modern societies. To claim abstractly that some remarkable change must come about in the future if democracy is to be realized, without showing why and how some specific human agents may possibly bring it about, violates the requirements of reflective thinking and forfeits any right to be taken seriously. Yet that is precisely the remarkably un-Deweyan claim Dewey asserted in *The Public and Its Problems*: a utopian end but no practical means to achieve it!

Essentially the same criticism has been made by one of Dewey's most perceptive admirers, Robert Westbrook. Though Westbrook uses softer language, he makes the same basic point. By ignoring the requirements of his own general theory of instrumental intelligence, of "how we think," Dewey inevitably failed to achieve his goal, namely, to combat effectively the antidemocratic "realist" ideas and movements that impelled him to write *The Public and Its Problems*. The following is Westbrook's devastating criticism:

Perhaps most troubling about the questions Dewey avoided in *The Public and Its Problems* is his own concession of their undeniable importance. As he said, it was essential to answer the question "By what means shall [the public's] inchoate and amorphous estate be organized into effective political action relevant to present social needs and opportunities?" Moreover, he was himself constantly railing against those who were guilty of wishful thinking because of an inattentiveness to means. A wish, he said, "becomes an aim or end only when it is worked out in terms of concrete conditions available for its realization, that is in terms of 'means.'" Much of what passed for moral ends, he complained, "do not get beyond the stage of fancy of something agreeable and desirable based upon an emotional wish. . . . Unless ideals are to be dreams and idealism a synonym for romanticism and phantasy-building, there must be a most realistic study of actual conditions and of the mode or law of natural events in order to give the imagined or ideal object definite form and solid substance— to give it, in short, practicality and constitute it a working end." Dewey's failure to constitute participatory democracy as a compelling "working end," as well as the demanding conditions he set for its realization, made *The Public and Its Problems* a less than effective counter to democratic realism. Too many questions were left unanswered.[22]

What is most astonishing—and regrettable—about Dewey's evasive sophistry in 1927 was his failure to recognize that in 1902 he already had, to a large extent, brilliantly provided a practical solution to the problem of constructing democratic, cosmopolitan, neighborly communities!

As noted in Chapter 2, Dewey's "The School as Social Centre" address to the National Educational Association had accelerated development of the community school movement then underway. Though not nearly as fully and as explicitly as stated here, that movement's basic aim was—and continues to be—to construct the democratic, cosmopolitan, neighborly communities needed to function as the organizational foundation of the participatory democratic society Dewey had envisioned as early as 1888.

After 1902, for reasons that are still baffling, Dewey seems to have almost completely dropped out of the community school movement, which episodically rose and fell throughout the twentieth century. Dewey's failure in 1927 to recognize the far-reaching implications of the ideas he had prophetically advocated in 1902 seems particularly ironic when we consider that shortly after 1927, his ideas about schools functioning as fundamentally strategic community social centers were implemented in real-world practice by his former student and continuing protégé, Elsie Clapp.

Elsie Clapp's Contributions to Community Schools

The work which is here described is itself a tribute to John Dewey, whose philosophy and whose vision of the school as a social institution prompted our efforts to create a community school and to participate in community education. Although he is in no way responsible for what was done, everything that we have learned from our experiences in this attempt we learned in a special sense from him.

—ELSIE CLAPP, *COMMUNITY SCHOOLS IN ACTION* (1939)

A S NOTED IN CHAPTER 2, in his 1902 address Dewey had not assigned the neighborhood school two sets of responsibilities:

1. To organize itself so that its resources of various kinds (e.g., staff, administrative skills, prestige, access to "influentials") could be used to solve specific neighborhood problems;
2. To organize its "day-school" curriculum and activities so as to engage its students in real-world community problem-solving (i.e., learning and knowing by means of action-oriented community problem-solving, which requires initiative, imagination, and collaboration).

Recognizing those responsibilities as logical extensions of Dewey's general theory, his protégé Elsie Clapp attempted to organize community schools that could provide something like the kind of collaborative, community problem-solving, instrumental education most likely to develop higher levels of instrumental intelligence in individuals, communities, and societies.

Dewey, of course, repeatedly called for instrumental education based on "learning by doing." But, as discussed previously, his Laboratory School was actually based on learning by simulated doing, not real-world community doing. Clapp's experimental schools went much further in the direction of putting Dewey's theory into practice than the Laboratory School did. The Clapp schools were much more Deweyan than the laboratory school.

From 1929 to 1936, Clapp organized and directed two experimental schools in rural communities. The first school, which she directed from 1929 to 1934, was the Ballard School in Jefferson County, Kentucky; the second, which she directed from 1934 to 1936, was in Arthurdale, West Virginia. She subsequently provided a detailed account of the two schools in a book published in 1939 entitled *Community Schools in Action*.[1] The book was designed to support this primary thesis: John Dewey's general theory of community schooling works in practice.

Clapp's introduction emphasized the extent to which she regarded the two community schools described in her book as practical demonstrations of Dewey's philosophy and theory of community schooling and education.

> The work which is here described is itself a tribute to John Dewey, whose philosophy and whose vision of the school as a social institution prompted our efforts to create a community school and to participate in community education. Although he is no way responsible for what was done, everything that we have learned from our experiences in this attempt we learned in a special sense from him. The work and the book which records it are to be counted among the numberless expressions of appreciation in this country and abroad of the greatest thinker of our time.[2]

Among other things, Dewey's four-page foreword to Clapp's book suggests the intellectual benefits he derived from reflecting (though not acting) on four decades of work by numerous "school reformers" since the 1902 publication of his address "The School as Social Centre" and his 1916 book, *Democracy and Education*. Dewey's foreword clarifies and extends not only his ideas about the symbiotic relationships between communities and schools but his revived emphasis on the importance of formal schools as well. It also unwittingly reveals the critical strategic error that has, until recently, worked against widespread implementation of the community school idea as the practical means to radically improve the American schooling system and to help construct the democratic, cosmopolitan, neighborly communities that Dewey correctly claimed were necessary for the progressive democratic reconstruction of American society.

Dewey wrote the foreword to help call "attention to the extraordinary significance for education of the work reported in this book." By 1939, as his foreword makes clear, Dewey had come to equate community education with education itself: "If I said the book is a record of a highly significant undertaking in the field of community education, it would sound as if schools had in addition some other field of operations. In fact they do not have. Miss Clapp remarks that 'a great deal is said in calling a school a community school.' If the school lives up to that name, everything is said."[3]

Dewey praised Clapp's book for clearly portraying what good community schools do and how they function. He only found it necessary, therefore, to "underline some points":

> Perhaps the first lesson it teaches is that schools function socially only when they function in a community for community purposes and communities are local, present, and close by, while "society" at large is something vaguely in the distance. . . . The neighborhood is the prime community; it certainly is so for the children and youth who are educated in the school, and it must be so for administrators and teachers if the idea of socially functioning schools is to take on flesh and blood. There is no occasion for fear that the local community

will not provide roads leading out into wider human relations if the opportunities it furnishes are taken advantage of.[4]

It is important to note that Dewey's point here was that local community schools need not function in ways that contribute to the development of parochial, ethnocentric communities. On the contrary, local need not entail parochial. Good community schools were possible and could powerfully help develop democratic, *cosmopolitan*, neighborly communities.

To underscore the community nature of the experimental schools described by Clapp, Dewey characterized them as

> school[s] to which Lincoln's words about democratic government apply, . . . school[s] not only for, but of and by the community; the teachers being leaders in the movement, since they are themselves so identified with the community. An important aspect of this point is that those who were teachers in the schools prepared themselves for their work by becoming citizen members of the community in the most intimate way. They became acquainted with their neighbors by being part of the neighborhood. They knew the other members in a face-to-face-way. They kept up all the time they were there this process of educating themselves as to the community's needs and resources, its weaknesses and strong points; they learned that only in this way could they engage in further education of the community. They did not "survey" the community; they belonged to it. Results proved the immeasurable value of this phase of community education.[5]

To help understand the post-1939 history of the community-school idea, however, we cannot overemphasize the point that Dewey's enthusiastic praise for Elsie Clapp's community schools was explicitly limited to schools in only one type of American community: the rural community, which was rapidly becoming uncharacteristic of American society. As the quotation below shows unequivocally, if

Dewey's argument were accepted as valid, the community school idea would really only be an exercise in nostalgia, a "looking backward" lament for the rapidly vanishing America of Dewey's youth in mid-nineteenth-century Burlington, Vermont.

> The way in which the subject-matter to be taught [in the Clapp schools] was selected and the way in which methods for teaching it grew directly out of knowledge of community conditions are so concretely reported in the pages of the book that I hardly need to underline the point. *I do wish to add from personal knowledge, however, that the vital responsiveness of the members of the community, young and old, to the school as a center of its own life is understated rather than exaggerated in the pages which follow. Closely connected with the warmth and extent of the response is the fact, I believe, that the community was a rural community* [emphasis added]. For I am convinced it is a mistake to believe that the most needed advances in school organization and activities are going to take place in cities, especially in large cities. *From the viewpoint of genuine community education, country districts provide the greatest opportunity as well as exhibit the most crying need—the most vocal even if not in fact the deepest* [emphasis added]. The connection of school activities with out-of-school activities is indirect in the city. It is immediate, close at hand, in villages where there are gardens, shops, and a variety of household activities to meet family needs.[6]

Unfortunately, Dewey's school dichotomy—rural community vs. large city—was not only radically false, but also had disastrous consequences for the post–World War II history of "community schools" and "community education" in general. Unwittingly, by using his great prestige to try to channel progressive educational programs and energies into rural schools and away from urban schools, Dewey significantly contributed to the post–World War II debacle of American schools and American cities. Rather than develop that argument at length here, however, Dewey's theoretically insightful concluding paragraph on the symbiotic relationships among communities, community problem-solving schools, and democracy is more useful for our purposes.

> Even at the risk of stating the obvious, I conclude by pointing out how central are the problems of health, recreation, and of occupations carried on for a livelihood in any community; how conspicuously these problems stand out in a rural community where they offer themselves as direct personal issues. But I want to point to the book as evidence of how the school as well as the community gains when these basic interests of life are made fundamental in education. I might also say that it is surprising how many alleged pedagogical problems relating to such matters as "discipline and freedom, motivation," etc., either vanish or are greatly reduced when a school is a living part of the community. I do not know that there is much danger that the social function of education will be thought of exclusively as the question of what schools could and should do for the community. But if there is any danger at all, the schools here reported show that the relation is a two-way process. *They prove what the community can do for schools when the latter are actually centers of community life. Here are cases in which communities develop themselves by means of schools which are centers of their own life. In consequence, there is no detail in the following report which will not repay study. The report is a demonstration in practice of the place of education in building a democratic life* [emphasis added].[7]

Dewey's foreword constitutes a bewildering mixture of brilliant insights and observations, radically false dichotomies and value judgments, and astonishing omissions. Despite its serious flaws, we can use it as a basis to show how, since 1985, we have logically extended the Dewey-Clapp theory of community schools to help develop a practical means to realize Dewey's inspiring vision of participatory democracy. To place our own work since 1985 in historical perspective, however, it seems useful to sketch some relevant aspects of the very loosely organized community-school "movement" before, during, and shortly after World War II.

Elsie Clapp's experimental schools were far from unique during the 1930s and 1940s. Spurred by the post-1929 Depression and wartime crises, schools in many American communities tried to develop solutions to local problems.[8] One of the most impressive experiments was inspired and facilitated by Maurice Seay, director of the Bureau of School Service at the University of Kentucky.

Maurice Seay and Community Schools

Making innovative use of funds provided by the Sloan Foundation, during the 1930s and early 1940s, under the direction of Maurice Seay, the University of Kentucky helped teachers throughout the state develop school-based programs to help solve local community problems. Understandably, therefore, when the highly influential National Society for the Study of Education planned its 1945 yearbook, *Curriculum Reconstruction for American Education in the Postwar Period*, Seay was chosen to write the chapter "The Community School Emphasis in Postwar Education."

Published in 1945, the yearbook's general purpose was "to provide the most serviceable guidance possible for the replanning of educational programs that will obviously be required to meet postwar demands upon the schools."[9] Perhaps reflecting the intellectual influence of Clapp and Dewey, and definitely reflecting the innovative work Seay had helped facilitate in Kentucky schools during the Depression and World War II, his chapter began by emphasizing that community schools had "two distinctive emphases—service to the entire community not merely to the children of school age, and discovery, development, and use of the resources of the community as part of the educational facilities of the school."[10]

To avoid the impression that community schools were designed to foster localism and parochialism, Seay emphasized their cosmopolitan orientation and their global concept of community: "The concern of the community school with the local community is intended, not to restrict the school's attention to local matters, but to provide a focus from which to relate study and action in the larger community—the state, the region, the nation, the world."[11]

To support his proposition that the "possibilities of a school's service to its community are almost limitless" and that "the community can serve its school in as many ways as the school can serve the community,"[12] Seay provided numerous and varied examples of collaborative and mutually beneficial school-community interaction throughout the country. The following are Seay's most insightful observations—observations that we believe are highly applicable to the contemporary movement for community schools:

> In addition to knowing children and the subject matter to be taught, teachers of schools which emphasize community resources must know the interests and the customs of the people whom they serve, their problems, and how they make a living. They must know the organizations and methods of the other public services of the community. They must know how the problems of their patrons and the agencies of the community relate to problems and agencies elsewhere in the state, in the nation, in the world. *Above all they must know how to study a local community so as to identify its problems and resources* [emphasis added].[13]

Directly contradicting Dewey's proposition in his foreword to Clapp's *Community Schools in Action*, Seay concluded the chapter by emphasizing the universal applicability of the community school idea.

> Finally, it will be noted that in this chapter the illustrations have been confined to rural and small urban communities. Although community education is more difficult to organize in a complex metropolitan area, the need for it is no less in large urban communities. The community-school emphasis has significance for postwar education in all communities.[14]

The Rise and Decline of the Community School Movement after 1945

As is well known, victory over Germany and Japan in World War II briefly resulted in a great deal of democratic optimism. For a few years, the community school idea significantly benefited from that optimism. Shortly after publication of its 1945 yearbook, the board of directors of the National Society for the Study of Education decided to publish an entire "yearbook on the current status and potentialities of the community school." For advice, the board "naturally turned to the author of the [stimulating] chapter" on postwar education from their 1945 yearbook and appointed Maurice Seay chairman of the yearbook committee on community schools.[15]

Published in 1953 as Part II of the Society's *Fifty-Second Yearbook* and entitled *The Community School*, that volume still constitutes the fullest and best exposition of the community school idea; it has powerfully influenced our work on Dewey and the American schooling system. Focused on "The Community School Defined," one chapter creatively develops the basic ideas Maurice Seay sketched in 1945. Noting the "variety of programs offered by community schools," the authors of the chapter present a "definition which is universal in scope and adaptable to any social, economic, or political setting." Their definition is as follows:

A community school is a school which has concerns beyond the training of literate, "right-minded," and economically efficient citizens who reflect the values and processes of a particular social, economic, and political setting. In addition to these basic educational tasks, it is *directly concerned with improving all aspects of living in the community* [original emphasis] in all the broad meaning of that concept, in the local, state, regional, national, or international community. To attain that end, the community school is *consciously used* [original emphasis] by the people of the community. Its curriculum reflects planning to meet the discovered needs of the community with changes in emphasis as circumstances indicate. Its buildings and physical facilities are at once a center for both youth and adults who together are actively engaged in analyzing problems suggested by the needs of the community and in formulating and exploring solutions to those problems. Finally, the community school is concerned that the people put solutions into operation to the end that living is improved and enriched for the individual and the community.[16]

The concluding chapter of *The Community School* volume was co-authored by Maurice Seay. Appropriately enough, by 1953 Seay had become chairman of the Department of Education at the University of Chicago, where a half-century earlier John Dewey had sketched his prophetic general theory of "The School as Social Centre." Though Seay's summary chapter, "Overcoming Barriers to The Development of Community Schools," did not specifically cite Dewey's theory, as the following quotation demonstrates, it was quintessentially Deweyan in its emphasis on the strongly symbiotic relationships among participatory democracy, community schools, and neighborly local communities:

> The community school program, in a very real sense, represents the essence of democracy. . . . The community school serves the community, and the community serves the school. Teachers, students, and citizens participate in planning the educational activities as well as taking part in them. Such a school is an integral part of the community; its program, in large measure, grows out of the community itself. Those who are interested in controlling the growing centralization of authority and power in state and federal government will find in community schools a counterbalance to that trend. In our world we shall continue to have great powers in state and national governments. Community schools give new vitality to communities and justify the hope of a desirable balance.[17]

With the benefit of hindsight, we can now see that publication of *The Community School* represented the high point of the post-1945 movement it advocated so enthusiastically. As John Puckett shows in detail in a recent book, for complex reasons—including the devastating impact of the cold war on democratic tendencies in American society and particularly its educational system—support for community schools rapidly declined after 1953.[18] In 1985, however, the University of Pennsylvania began working to revitalize the community school idea. To better suggest how and why that development came about, Part II of this book begins with a highly oversimplified sketch of American higher education since 1876.

 Part II

5 Penn and the Third Revolution in American Higher Education

Nothing is of more importance to the public weal, than to form and train up youth in wisdom and virtue. Wise and good men are, in my opinion, the strength of a state; much more so than riches or arms, which, under the management of Ignorance and Wickedness, often draw on destruction, instead of providing for the safety of a people.

BENJAMIN FRANKLIN TO SAMUEL JOHNSON (AUGUST 23, 1750)

AS EMPHASIZED IN CHAPTER 2, the president of the University of Chicago, William Rainey Harper, significantly helped John Dewey see the critically important role the schooling system must play in the development of a democratic American society. Unfortunately, Dewey's work on schools suffered badly from his failure to see what Harper saw so clearly, namely, that the research university must constitute the primary component of a highly integrated (pre-K–post 16) schooling system that could potentially function as the primary agent of democracy in the world and in the United States in particular. As we emphasized, Harper envisioned the university as the "prophet of democracy, its priest and its philoso pher . . . the Messiah of the democracy, its to-be-expected deliverer."[1]

Democracy is the soul of America—its charter myth, its ultimate end-in-view. The American university, alas, has never played anything like the messianic democratic role Harper optimistically envisioned for it. But "the times they are a-changin'" and our work since 1985 has been strongly influenced by our own optimistic belief that

Harper's vision may yet be realized. Does this optimistic belief show that we simply are suffering from a bad case of the delusionary utopianism long characteristic of American progressives and leftists? As we hope to soon illustrate, this is not the case.

Following Donald Kennedy's provocative lead in his book *Academic Duty*, we view American higher education today as in the early stages of its third revolution.[2] The first revolution, of course, occurred in the late nineteenth century. Beginning at Johns Hopkins in 1876, the accelerating adoption and uniquely American adaptation of the German model somewhat revolutionized American higher education. By the turn of the century, the American research university had essentially been created. The second revolution began in 1945 with Vannevar Bush's "endless [research] frontier" manifesto and rapidly produced the big science, cold war, entrepreneurial university.[3] We believe that the third revolution began in 1989. The fall of the Berlin Wall and the end of the cold war provided the necessary conditions for the "revolutionary" emergence of the democratic, cosmopolitan, civic university—the radically new type of "great university," which William Rainey Harper had prophesized would advance democratic schooling and achieve practical realization of the democratic promise of America for all Americans.

The emergence of the new type of university a century after Harper had first envisioned it can be credibly explained as a defensive response to the increasingly obvious, increasingly embarrassing, increasingly immoral contradiction between the status, wealth, and power of American higher education—particularly its elite research university component—and the pathological state of American cities.

To paraphrase Oliver Goldsmith's late eighteenth-century lament for the *Deserted Village*, while American research universities flourished in the late twentieth century as never before, "ill-fared the American city, to hastening ills a prey." If American research universities really were so great, why were American cities so pathological? After the cold war ended, the contradiction became increasingly obvious, troubling, indefensible, and immoral. The manifest contradiction between the power and the performance of American higher education sparked the emergence of the *truly* (not simply rhetorically) engaged university and the growing acceptance of the proposition that power based on a great capacity for integrated production and use of knowledge should mean responsible performance. In the aftermath of the cold war, accelerating external and internal pressures forced research universities to recognize (very reluctantly) that they must—and could—function as moral/intellectual institutions simultaneously engaged in advancing universal knowledge, learning, *and* improving the well-being of their local geographic communities (i.e., the local ecological systems that powerfully affect their own health and functioning). We believe that after 1989 the combination of external pressure and enlightened self-interest spurred American research universities to increasingly recognize that they could, indeed must, function simultaneously as universal and local institutions of higher education—institutions not only *in* but *for* their local communities.

To reduce, if not avoid, misunderstanding, we emphasize that we view the "third revolution" as still in its early—very early—stages. As the old academic joke has it, universities constitute such remarkably fragmented, self-contradictory, internally competitive and conflictual institutions that they tend to move with all the speed of a runaway glacier. But things are changing in the right direction. One indicator of positive change is the accelerating number and variety of universities and colleges (i.e., "higher eds," a less cumbersome term than "higher educational institutions" or "postsecondary institutions") that now publicly proclaim their desire to collaborate actively with their neighboring public schools and local communities. Predictably to date, public proclamations of collaboration far surpass tangible, interactive, mutually respectful and beneficial collaboration, but progress is being made.

To help accelerate progress to the point where major changes become firmly institutionalized and produce significant results, we call for action-oriented acceptance of this radical proposition: all higher eds should explicitly make solving the problem of the American schooling system a very high institutional priority; their contributions to its solution should count heavily both in assessing their institutional performance and in responding to their requests for renewed or increased financial support. Actively helping to develop an effective, integrated, genuinely democratic, pre-K through higher education schooling system, we contend, should become a collaborative primary mission of American universities and colleges.

Primary mission does not mean sole mission. Obviously, American higher eds now have—and will continue to have—important missions other than collaboratively helping to solve the problems of the American schooling system. If we had unlimited space, we would try to show in great detail how those other missions would benefit greatly from successful collaborative work on the schooling problem. Here we restrict ourselves to a barebones statement of two corollary propositions:

1. Solving the overall problem of the schooling system must begin with changes at the higher education level.
2. Solving the overall schooling-system problem would, in the long run, both directly and indirectly, give higher eds much greater resources than they now have to carry out *all* of their important missions.

In the short term, we concede, our proposed mission change would require higher eds to experience the trauma entailed by any attempt to change academic priorities, structures, and cultures radically. We are calling on these institutions to reallocate a very large share of their intellectual (among other) resources to the immediate improvement of their neighboring public schools and communities. Given their present ferociously competitive "pure research" orientation, how in the world can we possibly expect universities to answer our call positively rather than contemptuously? Since they themselves are not experiencing any crisis, why should self-congratulatory, increasingly rich, prestigious, powerful, "successful" American research universities undertake the terribly difficult job of trying to transform themselves into engaged civic institutions that actively and wholeheartedly accept reciprocal and mutually respectful collaboration with their local schools and communities as a very high priority for the new millennium? They should try to do so for strong institutional reasons: if they succeed, they will be much better able than they are now to achieve their self-professed, loudly trumpeted, traditional missions, these missions being to advance, preserve, and transmit knowledge, *and* they will help produce the well-educated, cultured, truly democratic citizens necessary to develop and maintain a genuinely democratic society.[4]

We think it axiomatic that universities—particularly elite research universities with highly selective arts and sciences colleges—function as the primary shapers of the overall American schooling system. We think it equally axiomatic that, in the global era, the schooling system increasingly functions as the core subsystem—the strategic subsystem—of modern information societies. Contrary to the position taken by orthodox Marxist ideologists, more than any other subsystem, it now influences the functioning of the societal system as a whole. Viewed systemically, on balance it has the greatest "multiplier" effects, both direct and indirect, as well as short and long term.

To understate the case extravagantly, to fully develop the demo-cratic, cosmopolitan, civic university dedicated to, actively engaged in, and pragmatically capable of solving the problem of the overall American schooling system will be extraordinarily hard. There is a great deal to think about, figure out, and do. Among many other things, to fully develop that new type of American university will require countering and displacing the now dominant big science, cold war, entrepreneurial university strategy with a more compelling, morally inspiring, and *intelligent* strategy. Since 1985, we have been trying to contribute concretely to the complex process of developing such a strategy by following brilliant leads provided by William Rainey Harper, John Dewey, and many others. We have stood on their shoulders and consciously tried to integrate, realize, and progress beyond their combined visions.

Increasing Penn's Engagement with Local Public Schools as a Practical Example of Democratic Devolution Revolution

Since 1985, the University of Pennsylvania has increasingly engaged itself with its local public schools in a comprehensive school-commu-nity-university partnership that was initially known as the West

Philadelphia Improvement Corps (WEPIC). In its more than twenty years of operation, the project has evolved significantly. Moreover, it has helped spawn a variety of related projects that also engage Penn with public schools in its local community, West Philadelphia. From its inception, we conceptualized Penn's work with WEPIC as designed to forge mutually beneficial and respectful university-school-community partnerships. In recent years, we have begun to conceptualize that work in much broader terms, namely, as part of a literally radical attempt to advance a "democratic devolution revolution."[5] It is from that lofty perch that an overview of Penn's work—and the work of many other higher educational institutions engaged with their local public schools—is best comprehended.

John Gardner, arguably the leading spokesperson for the "New Democratic Cosmopolitan Civic University" (our term for it), thought and wrote about organizational devolution and the university's potential role for nearly a generation. For him, the effective functioning of organizations required the planned and deliberate rather than haphazard devolution of functions.

> We have in recent decades discovered some important characteristics of the large-scale organized systems—government, private sector, whatever—under which so much of contemporary life is organized. One such characteristic—perhaps the most important—is that the tendency of such systems to centralize must be countered by deliberate dispersion of initiative downward and outward through the system. The corporations have been trying to deal with this reality for almost 25 years and government is now pursuing it. . . . What it means for government is a substantially greater role for the states and cities. And none of them are entirely ready for that role. . . . Local government must enter into collaborative relations with non-governmental elements. . . . So how can colleges and universities be of help?[6]

Gardner powerfully extended the Harper-Dewey vision by proposing a multisided involvement in "contemporary life" for higher eds, including initiating community building, convening public discussions, educating public-spirited leaders, offering continuing civic and leadership seminars, and providing a wide range of technical assistance. The effective, compassionate, democratic devolution revolution we call for requires much more than practicing new forms of interaction among federal, state, and local governments and among agencies at each level of government; it requires, to use Gardner's phrase, "the deliberate dispersion of initiative downward and outward through the system." For Gardner, government integration by itself does not make meaningful change. New forms of interaction among the public, for-profit, and nonprofit sectors are also mandatory. Government must function as a collaborating partner, effectively facilitating cooperation among all sectors of society, including higher educational institutions, to support and strengthen individuals, families, and communities.[7]

An Innovative Strategy to Achieve a Democratic Devolution Revolution

To extend Gardner's observations about universities and colleges (and similar observations by such highly influential thinkers as Ernest Boyer, Derek Bok, Lee Shulman, and Alexander Astin), we propose a democratic devolution revolution.[8] In our proposed "revolution," government serves as a powerful catalyst and largely provides the funds needed to create stable, ongoing, effective partnerships. But government would function only as a *second tier deliverer of services*, with higher eds, community-based organizations, unions, churches, other voluntary associations, school children and their parents, and other community members functioning as the first-tier operational partners. That is, various levels and departments of government would guarantee aid and significantly finance welfare services. Local personalized-care services, however, would actually be delivered by the third tier (private, nonprofit, voluntary associations) and fourth tier (personal—family, kin, neighbors, friends) of society. Government would not be primarily responsible for the delivery of services; it would instead have macrofiscal responsibilities, including fully adequate provision of funds.

The strategy we propose requires creatively and intelligently adapting the work and resources of a wide variety of local institutions (e.g., higher eds, hospitals, faith-based organizations) to the particular needs and resources of local communities. It assumes, however, that universities and colleges, which simultaneously constitute preeminent international, national, and local institutions, *potentially* represent by far the most powerful partners, "anchors," and creative catalysts for change and improvement in the quality of life in American cities and communities.

For universities and colleges to fulfill their great potential and really contribute to a democratic devolution revolution, they will have to do things very differently than they do now. To begin with, changes in "doing" will require recognition by higher eds that, as they now function, they—particularly universities—constitute a major part of the problem, not a significant part of the solution. To become part of the solution, higher eds must give full-hearted, full-minded devotion to the painfully difficult task of transforming themselves into socially responsible *civic universities and colleges*. To do so, they will have to radically change their institutional cultures and structures, democratically realign and integrate themselves, and develop a comprehensive, realistic strategy.

The major component of the neo-Deweyan strategy now being developed and slowly implemented by Penn focuses on developing *university-assisted community schools* designed to help educate, engage, activate, and serve *all* members of the community in which the school is located. The strategy assumes that community schools, like higher eds, can function as focal points to help create healthy urban environments and that both universities and colleges function best in such environments. Somewhat more specifically, the strategy assumes that, like higher eds, public schools can function as environment-changing institutions and can become the strategic centers of broadly based partnerships that genuinely engage a wide variety of community organizations and institutions. As Dewey, Clapp, and Seay emphasized, since public schools "belong" to all members of the community, they should "serve" all members of the community. (No implication is intended that public schools are the only community places where learning takes place. Obviously, it also takes place in libraries, museums, private schools, et cetera. Ideally, all the "learning places" in a community would collaborate.)

More than any other institution, public schools are particularly well suited, therefore, to function as neighborhood "hubs" or "centers," around which local partnerships can be generated and developed. When they play that innovative role, schools function as community institutions *par excellence*. They then provide a decentralized, democratic, community-based response to rapidly changing community problems. In the process, they help young people learn better, at increasingly higher levels, through action-oriented, collaborative, real-world problem solving.

For public schools to actually function as integrating community institutions, however, local, state, and national governmental and nongovernmental agencies must be effectively coordinated to help provide the myriad resources community schools need to play the greatly expanded roles we envision them playing in American society. How to conceive that organizational revolution, let alone implement it, poses extraordinarily complex intellectual and social problems. But as Dewey forcefully argued, working to solve complex, real-world problems is the best way to advance knowledge and learning, as well as the *general capacity* of individuals and institutions to advance knowledge and learning.

We contend, therefore, that American universities should give a high priority—arguably their highest priority—to solving the problems inherent in the organizational revolution we have sketched above. If universities were to do so, they would demonstrate in concrete practice their self-professed theoretical ability to simultaneously advance knowledge and learning. They would then satisfy the critical performance test proposed in 1994 by the president of the State University of New York at Buffalo, William R. Greiner, namely, that *"the great universities of the twenty-first century will be judged by their ability to help solve our most urgent social problems* [emphasis added]."[9]

Since 1985, to increase Penn's ability to help solve America's most urgent social problems, we have worked to develop and implement the idea of university-assisted community schools. We emphasize *university-assisted* because community schools require far more resources than traditional schools do and because we have become convinced that universities constitute the strategic sources of broadly based, comprehensive, sustained support for community schools.

The university-assisted community school idea we have been developing at Penn since 1985 essentially extends and updates the Dewey-Clapp-Seay theory that the neighborhood school can function as the core neighborhood institution—the core institution which provides comprehensive services, galvanizes other community institutions and groups, helps solve the myriad problems communities confront in a rapidly changing world, and thereby actively helps construct the "organic" society Dewey theoretically envisioned in 1888. Dewey recognized that if the neighborhood school were to function as a genuine community center, it needed additional human resources and support. But to our knowledge, he never identified universities as *the* (or even *a*) key source of broadly based, sustained, comprehensive support for community schools.

In Chapter 6 we illustrate how university-assisted community schools can contribute to an effective democratic devolution revolution capable of helping to achieve Dewey's vision of participatory democracy. It is critical to emphasize, however, that the university-assisted community schools now being developed have a very long way to go before they can effectively mobilize the potentially powerful, untapped resources of their communities and thereby enable individuals and families to function as community problem-solvers, as well as deliverers and recipients of caring, compassionate, local services. The "narrative history" of our experience at Penn suggests both how far we have come and how far we have to go.

Penn and West Philadelphia Public Schools: Learning by Reflective Doing

Following the brilliant leads provided by Harper, Dewey, Gardner, and others, we believe that, as is true of all American universities, Penn's highest, most basic, and most enduring responsibility is to help

America realize in concrete practice the egalitarian promise of the Declaration of Independence: America will become an optimally democratic society, the pathbreaking democratic society in an increasingly interdependent world, the exemplary democratic model for the improvement of the human condition. Once that proposition is granted, the problem then becomes, how can Penn best fulfill its democratic responsibility? We believe it can best do so by effectively integrating and radically improving the entire West Philadelphia schooling system, beginning with Penn but comprehending *all* schools within West Philadelphia, the university's local geographic community.

The history of Penn's work with West Philadelphia public schools, we confess, has been a process of painful organizational learning and conflict; we cannot overemphasize that we have made many mistakes and our understanding and activities have continually changed over time.[10] Moreover, Penn is only now beginning to tap its extraordinary resources in ways that eventually could mutually benefit both Penn and its neighbors and result in truly radical school, community, and university change. Significantly, we have come to see our work as a concrete example of Dewey's general theory of learning by means of action-oriented, collaborative, real-world problem solving. Conceptualizing our work in terms of schools as the strategic components of complex urban ecological systems represented a major advance for us.

When we first began work on university-community relationships in 1985, we did not envision it in terms of schools or universities as highly strategic components of urban ecological systems. What immediately concerned us was that West Philadelphia was rapidly and visibly deteriorating, with devastating consequences for Penn. Given that "present situation" (as Dewey would have phrased it), what should the university do? Committed to undergraduate teaching, we designed an Honors Seminar, which aimed to stimulate undergraduates to think critically about what Penn could and should do to remedy its "environmental situation." For a variety of reasons, the president of the university, Sheldon Hackney, himself a former professor of history, agreed to join us in giving that seminar in the spring semester of 1985. The seminar's title suggests its general concerns: "Urban University-Community Relationships: Penn-West Philadelphia, Past, Present, and Future as a Case Study."

When the seminar began, we didn't know anything about Dewey's community school ideas. We literally knew nothing about the history of community school experiments and had not given any thought to Penn working with public schools in West Philadelphia. For present purposes, we need not recite the complex and painful process of trial, error, and failure that led us—and our students—to see that Penn's best strategy to remedy its rapidly deteriorating environmental situation was to use its enormous internal and external resources to help radically improve both West Philadelphia public schools *and* the neighborhoods in which they are located. Most unwittingly, during the course of the seminar's work, we reinvented the community school idea!

We came to realize, more or less accidentally, that public schools, if strongly assisted by Penn, could effectively function as genuine community centers for the organization, education, and transformation of entire neighborhoods. They could do so by functioning as neighborhood sites for a West Philadelphia Improvement Corps (WEPIC), consisting of school personnel and neighborhood residents who would receive strategic assistance from Penn students, faculty, and staff in their efforts to improve their schools and their quality of life. The seminar helped invent WEPIC to help transform the traditional West Philadelphia public school system into a "revolutionary" new collaborative system of university-assisted, community-centered, action-oriented, community problem-solving schools.

Given Penn's deep-rooted institutional resistance to serious involvement with West Philadelphia's problems, the limited resources available to us, and the intrinsic difficulty of transforming conventional, inner-city public schools into community schools, we decided that our best strategy was to try to achieve a visible, dramatic success in one school rather than marginal, incremental changes in a number of schools. That decision led us to concentrate initially on the John P. Turner Middle School, largely because of its principal's interest and leadership.

Previous experiments in community schools and community education throughout the country depended primarily on a single university unit, namely, the School of Education. This was one major reason, we were convinced, for the failure, or limited success at best, of those experiments. The WEPIC concept of university assistance to school *and* neighborhood was far more comprehensive. From the start of the Turner experiment, we envisioned the concept to mean assistance from, and mutually beneficial collaboration with, the entire range of Penn's schools, departments, institutes, centers, and administrative offices. For a variety of reasons, however, it soon became apparent that the best way to initiate and sustain the Turner project would be to begin with a school-based community health program.

Given the development of a community health program at Turner in the summer of 1990, Professor Francis Johnston, chair of the anthropology department and a world leader in nutritional anthropology, decided to participate in the project. To do so effectively, for the fall semester of 1990 he revised Anthropology 210 to focus on the relationship between nutrition and obesity, and to make it what we have come to call an action-oriented, strategic problem-solving, academically based community service seminar.[11] Anthropology 210 had a long history at Penn and focused on the complex connections between anthropology and biomedical science. An undergraduate course, it was developed to link premedical training at Penn with the Department of Anthropology's major program in medical anthropology. Premed students are very important in Penn's undergraduate education and the department's program in medical anthropology was world renowned. Professor Johnston's decision to convert Anthropology 210 into an academically based community service seminar designed to improve the nutritional knowledge and behavior of West Philadelphia students and residents constituted a major milestone in the development of the Turner community school program, in Penn's relationships with the Turner School, and in our overall work with West Philadelphia public schools and local neighborhoods. To suggest the significant benefits both Penn and West Philadelphia derive from academically based community service seminars and courses, we now briefly indicate how Anthropology 210 functioned after its reorientation and reorganization.

Over the past sixteen years, students in Anthropology 210 and its successor course, Anthropology 310, have been encouraged to view their education at Penn as preparing them to contribute to the solution of societal problems through service to and with the local community. To help them do so efficiently, in 1990 the inaugural seminar of Johnston's revised course focused on the strategic problem of improving the nutrition of disadvantaged inner-city children. And to help solve that problem, Anthropology 210 students worked with Turner teachers and students to design, construct, and operate a real-world "nutrition laboratory" in West Philadelphia.

Among its other goals, the "laboratory" was designed to improve the nutrition of Turner students—and their families—by providing them with a comprehensive, action-oriented framework for making informed decisions about diet, nutrition, and health. To help achieve that goal, Penn students worked closely with Turner students and teachers to carry out a variety of projects conveniently grouped into five main categories:

1. Teaching nutrition
2. Evaluating nutritional status (i.e., measuring over time the height, weight, and body mass of Turner students)
3. Recording and evaluating the students' actual diets
4. Interviewing family members
5. Reviewing nutritional ecology (i.e., observing behavior in the school lunchroom, mapping the various sources of food in the Turner neighborhood and the types of food promoted and sold in them)

To carry out these projects, Penn and Turner students collaboratively engaged in activities that required systematic reading and research, data collection, and data analysis and interpretation. That is, exemplifying the validity of John Dewey's general theory of effective learning by collaborative, constructive, real-world doing, Penn and Turner students learned by working to solve a strategic real-world problem and then *reflecting* on what they had done to solve that problem. As a result, Johnston found that Anthropology 210 worked better for Penn students than it ever had previously and the Turner students were highly motivated to work intensively on the subjects involved in the nutrition project. Moreover, he not only found the seminar continually more stimulating, enlightening, and enjoyable to teach, he also discovered that it significantly contributed to his own scholarly research.

To carry out the nutrition project, it was necessary for Penn undergraduates and Turner middle school students to collect, organize, and interpret a relatively large and complex body of data directly relevant to Johnston's longstanding research interests. In the process of carrying out their work, the Penn and Turner students functioned as research assistants to Johnston—as *collaborating* members of a research team supervised and directed by him. The data they produced proved so interesting and significant, in fact, that they became the main basis of a pathbreaking article he published in an academic journal, the *American Journal of Human Biology*. Entitled "Physical Growth, Nutritional Status, and Dietary Intake of African American Middle School Students from Philadelphia," Johnston's publication strongly supported the general proposition that has guided our own work on universities and community schools. The proposition asserts that the development of university-assisted community schools that effectively use academically based community service seminars and courses to help solve strategic community problems not only constitute practical means for the advancement of *learning* at different levels of schooling, they also constitute practical means for the advancement of *knowledge* by university professors and their local partners.

Since 1990, as the program evolved and demonstrably produced nutritional and educational benefits, students in Anthropology 210 and their numerous successors have carried out a variety of activities at Turner and other Penn-assisted community schools that focus on the causes and consequences of obesity and the interactive relationships among diet, nutrition, growth, and health. Increasingly, the program has been organized around academically based community service and collaborative real-world problem solving as a powerful strategy to improve Penn, public schools, and local neighborhoods. After Johnston began to focus his own research and publications on his work with Turner students and community residents to prevent or reduce obesity, he increasingly came to function as a noteworthy example for other anthropology professors and graduate students, who integrated their teaching and research with university-assisted community schools across West Philadelphia. Even more significantly, Anthropology 210 not only affected the anthropology department, which has developed a program in public interest anthropology,[12] its success radiated out to other departments and schools. Undoubtedly, it (and Johnston) has played major roles in the successful campaign to expand strategic academically based community service at Penn.[13]

At present, approximately 150 such courses, working with schools and community organizations to solve strategic community problems, have been developed at Penn, with 53 being offered during the 2005–2006 academic year. Moreover, an increasing number of faculty members, from a wide range of Penn schools and departments, are now seriously considering how they might revise existing courses, or develop new courses that would enable their students to benefit from innovative curricular opportunities to become active learners, creative real-world problem solvers, and active producers, not simply passive consumers, of knowledge. That relatively rapid growth has largely resulted from the organizational innovation described in Chapter 6.

The Center for Community
Partnerships

*The University and the City are important to one
another. We stand on common ground, our futures
very much intertwined.*

SHELDON HACKNEY, *PRESIDENT'S ANNUAL REPORT*
(1987–1988)

ENCOURAGED BY THE SUCCESS of the university's increasing engagement with West Philadelphia, in July 1992 President Hackney created the Center for Community Partnerships. To highlight the importance he attached to the center, he located it in the office of the president and appointed Ira Harkavy to be its director, while Harkavy continued to serve as director of the Penn Program for Public Service, created in 1988 in the School of Arts and Sciences. Symbolically and practically, creation of the center constituted a major change in Penn's relationship with West Philadelphia and the city as a whole. In principle, by creating the center, the university formally committed itself as a corporate entity to finding ways to use its truly enormous resources (e.g., student and faculty "human capital") to help improve the quality of life in its local community—not only in respect to public schools but to *economic and community development in general.*

The center is based on the assumption that one highly effective and efficient way for Penn to simultaneously serve its enlightened institutional self-interest and carry out its academic missions of advancing universal knowledge and educating students is to function as a *truly engaged*, democratic, cosmopolitan, civic university. It assumes that Penn's research and teaching should strongly focus on strategic universal problems—such as schooling, healthcare, and economic development—as these universal problems *manifest themselves locally in West Philadelphia and the rest of the city.* By focusing on strategic universal problems and effectively integrating general theory and concrete practice, as Benjamin Franklin advocated in the eighteenth century, Penn would symbiotically improve both the quality of life in its ecological community *and* its academic research and teaching.

The center is based on the proposition that when Penn is creatively conceived as a community-engaged civic university, it constitutes, in the best sense, both a universal and a local institution of higher education. As we optimistically envisioned it functioning, the Center for Community Partnerships would constitute a far-reaching innovation in university organization. To help overcome the remarkably competitive fragmentation that had developed after 1945, as Penn became a very large research university, the center would identify, mobilize, and integrate Penn's vast resources that could be used to help transform traditional West Philadelphia public schools into innovative community schools.

The emphasis on partnerships in the center's name was deliberate; it acknowledged that Penn could not try to go it alone in West Philadelphia as it had arrogantly been long accustomed to do. The creation of the center was also significant internally. It meant that, at least in principle, the president of the university would have—and use—an organizational vehicle to strongly encourage all components of the university to seriously consider the roles they could appropriately play in Penn's efforts to improve the quality of its off-campus environment. Implementation of that strategy accelerated after Judith Rodin became president in 1994. A native West Philadelphian and Penn graduate, Rodin was appointed in part because of her deeply felt commitment to improving Penn's local environment and to transforming Penn into *the* leading urban American university.

On taking office, Rodin made it her first priority to reform undergraduate education. To achieve that goal, she established the Provost's Council on Undergraduate Education and charged it with designing a model for Penn's undergraduate experience in the twenty-first century. Following the lead of Penn's patron saint, Benjamin Franklin, the Provost's Council emphasized the action-oriented union of theory and practice as well as "engagement with the material, ethical, and moral concerns of society and community defined broadly, globally, and also locally within Philadelphia." The Provost's Council defined the twenty-first century undergraduate experience as, "provid[ing] opportunities for students to understand what it means to be active learners and active citizens. It will be an experience of learning, knowing and doing that will lead to the active involvement of students in the process of their education."[1] To apply that Franklin-inspired orientation in practice, the Provost's Council designated academically based community service as a core component of Penn undergraduate education during the next century.

Building on themes identified by the Provost's Council, Penn's 1994–1995 annual report was entitled *The Unity of Theory and Practice: Penn's Distinctive Character*. Describing the university's efforts to integrate theory and practice, President Rodin observed that

> there are ways in which the complex interrelationships between theory and practice transcend any effort at neat conceptualization. One of those is the application of theory in service to our community and the use of community service as an academic research activity for students. *Nowhere else is the interactive dimension of theory and practice so clearly captured* [emphasis added].
>
> For more than 250 years, Philadelphia has rooted Penn in a sense of the "practical," reminded us that service to humanity, to our community is, as [Benjamin] Franklin put it, "the great aim and end of all learning." Today, thousands of Penn faculty and students realize the unity of theory and practice by engaging West Philadelphia elementary and secondary school students as part of their own academic course work in disciplines as diverse as history, anthropology, classical studies, education, and mathematics.

For example, anthropology Professor Frank Johnston and his undergraduate students educate students at West Philadelphia's Turner Middle School about nutrition. Classical studies professor Ralph Rosen uses modern Philadelphia and fifth-century-B.C. Athens to explore the interrelations between community, neighborhood, and family. And history professor Michael Zuckerman's students engage West Philadelphia elementary and secondary school students to help them understand together the nature—and discontinuities—of American national identity and national character.[2]

The 1994–1995 annual report illustrated and advanced a fundamental, far-reaching cultural shift that had *begun* to take place across the university. By the end of her first year in office, Penn's president had increased the prominence of undergraduate education, defined the integration of theory and practice (including theory and practice derived from and applied within the local community) as the hallmark of Benjamin Franklin's university, and identified academically based community service focused on West Philadelphia and its public schools and neighborhoods as a powerfully integrative strategy to advance university-wide research, teaching, and service.

Presidents can provide leadership, but it is faculty members who develop and sustain the courses and research projects that durably link a university to its local schools and community. More specifically, it is through faculty teaching and research that the connection to local schools and communities is ultimately made. Penn gave high priority, therefore, to increasing the number and variety of academically based community service courses.

Changing Penn's Undergraduate Curriculum to Help Change West Philadelphia's Public Schools

As a result of the highly positive reaction to those courses, the long-term process of changing Penn's undergraduate curriculum has accelerated. In addition to the development of the public interest anthropology track cited above, after years of complex negotiations, an interdisciplinary minor in urban education was created and hailed by undergraduates. A joint program of the School of Arts and Sciences (SAS) and the Graduate School of Education (GSE), the new minor included faculty advisors from across the SAS and the GSE. Appropriately enough, in the Fall 1998 issue of the SAS alumni publication, which focused on the urban crisis, Dean Samuel Preston voiced his strong support for the urban education minor, as well as for increasing the number of academically based community service courses:

> Together with the Graduate School of Education, SAS is offering a new interdisciplinary minor in Urban Education. The minor explores the crisis in public education in course work, in field research, and in hands-on study that uses the network of neighborhood schools the University has developed. SAS has been closely involved with the West Philadelphia community through Penn's Center for Community Partnerships. A number of our faculty focus their research on Philadelphia communities and regularly teach courses that put our students in touch with students at local schools. Penn students join with the students from surrounding neighborhoods to gather data, conduct interviews, and explore community problems such as inadequate nutrition or the presence of lead or toxins in homes. These service learning courses are one way that Penn mobilizes its academic resources in mutually beneficial partnerships with its neighbors. Surveys have shown that students are enthusiastic about how community service experiences enrich their Penn undergraduate education. *Arts and Sciences aims to develop more of these service learning approaches to education because of their value to students and their benefits to the community* [emphasis added].[3]

The dean of the college, Richard Beeman, enthusiastically echoed Dean Preston's support. Beeman, an early American historian and our longtime friend and colleague, had previously been openly skeptical of the value of academically based community service at a major research university. But in a spring 1998 speech to faculty and students, "Academically Based Community Service: From Skeptic to Convert," he publicly "confessed" that he had undergone something like a mind-and-spirit "conversion" experience. Translating his "personal conversion" into "institutional action," Dean Beeman initiated development of a pilot program within the College of Arts and Sciences in which problem-solving learning and academically based community service functioned as central components. He explained,

> I really cannot tell you how much I believe in the value of what is being done in those courses. They give our students a problem-oriented experience in learning, and all the research literature shows that the best learning takes place, not in studying theories and abstract forms, but in solving concrete problems. *I am committed to getting first rate faculty involved in that effort as an important definition of their contribution to undergraduate education at Penn* [emphasis added].[4]

In July 2003, Rebecca Bushnell succeeded Richard Beeman as dean of the college. (She became the dean of the SAS in 2005.) Bushnell, a scholar of Renaissance English literature and humanism, had been a strong supporter of academically based community service and problem-solving learning as associate dean of arts and letters, a position she held from 1998–2003. In a fall 2004 keynote address to an international conference held at Penn (and sponsored by "Imagining America," a consortium "linking universities with the communities they serve through arts and humanities projects"), Bushnell powerfully explained why as dean of the college "she believe[s] in the importance of making connections, through the arts and humanities, between artists, scholars and communities."

> Selfishly, I think Penn students have so much to learn from engagement in the work and from the dialogue that

undergirds these connections. I also think that they have a lot to learn about the process of the creation of knowledge in a democratic society. . . .

The premise of Imagining America . . . is to explore how, through making cultural connections, . . . [we can both] reproduce the spirit of the humanist classroom . . . [and] the democratic classroom in communities across America through the creation of art and ideas. . . . Knowledge is not packaged and delivered by universities either to their students or to the public at large; knowledge is made in the world, in the end, and for the world, as much in art as it is in science. Universities engage multiple partners in the production of knowledge, and we cannot erect a barrier between universities and communities in that process. We are, in short, all in this together.[5]

The SAS is only one of several Penn schools that, in recent years, have strengthened their connection with West Philadelphia public schools. In a variety of complex—and expensive—ways, Penn's institutional commitment has dramatically increased.

But as we have previously emphasized, Penn's increasing engagement with West Philadelphia represents far more than a philanthropic enterprise. It represents part of an evolving strategy to overcome—or at least significantly reduce—the competitive fragmentation accompanying Penn's transformation after 1945 into a rapidly expanding major research university. Perhaps the best way to show how that strategy works in practice is to describe a recent project designed both to "do good" and to help realize Penn's "One University" idea.

Community Healthcare as a Complex Strategic Problem to "Do Good" and Help Bring about "One University"

Penn is perhaps the only major American university where all of its schools and colleges are located on a contiguous urban campus. In the early 1970s, Martin Meyerson, the newly appointed president of the university, emphasized the extraordinary intellectual and social benefits that would result if the university took optimum advantage of the ease of interaction that a single campus location provides. To realize those benefits, he called for implementation of a "One University" organizational realignment—in which Penn would be characterized by intellectual collaboration and synergy across departments, divisions, colleges, and schools that would result in powerful advances in knowledge and human welfare.

That kind of radical realignment, of course, is much easier said than done. In practice, overcoming Penn's disciplinary fragmentation and conflict, narrow specialization, bureaucratic barriers, and what Benjamin Franklin had stigmatized in 1789 as "ancient Customs and Habitudes,"[6] proved enormously difficult to achieve; the "One University" idea essentially remained an idea, not a program of action. However, given the recent recognition that improving the health of urban communities is among the most significant problems confronting American society, it seemed possible to use it to resurrect the "One University" idea; solutions to the highly complex urban healthcare problem obviously require interschool and interdisciplinary collaboration. And that indeed proved to be the case when a school-based community healthcare project began at a West Philadelphia public school.

In recent years, it has been increasingly recognized that lack of accessible, effective healthcare is one of the most serious problems affecting poor urban communities. In fact, since we began work in 1985, West Philadelphia community leaders have identified improving healthcare as a critical need. And since the late 1980s, we have been trying—largely unsuccessfully—to develop a sustainable, comprehensive, effective healthcare program at local public schools. These efforts took a very positive turn in the spring and summer of 2002, when a group of undergraduates in our academically based community service seminar focused their research and service on helping to solve the healthcare crisis in West Philadelphia.

From their research, the students were well aware that community-oriented primary-care projects frequently flounder because of an inability to sustain adequate external funding. They concluded that for a school-based community healthcare project to be successfully sustained it had to be built into the curriculum at both the university and the public school. Only then would it gain a degree of permanence and stability. They proposed to create such a program at a local school—one that would serve as an easily accessible teaching and learning focal point for medical, dental, nursing, arts and sciences, social work, education, fine arts, and business students who would produce tangible, measurable, testable data and results. Their proposal proved to be so compelling that it led to the development of a school-based Community Health Promotion and Disease Prevention Program at Sayre Middle School. It is worth noting that one of the undergraduates who developed the Sayre project, Mei Elsanary, received the 2003 Swearer Humanitarian Award, given by Campus Compact to students for outstanding public service.

The school-based Community Health Promotion and Disease Prevention Program at Sayre Middle School was formally launched in January of 2003. It currently functions as the central component of a university-assisted community school designed both to advance student learning and democratic development, as well as to help strengthen families and institutions within the community. A community school is an ideal location for healthcare programs; it is not only where children learn but also where community members gather and participate in a variety of activities. Moreover, the multidisciplinary character of the Sayre Health Promotion and Disease Prevention Program enables it to be integrated into the curriculum and co-curriculum of both the public school and the university, assuring an educational focus as well as sustainability for the program. To support this aim, Penn faculty and students in medicine, nursing, dentistry, social work, arts and sciences, and fine arts, as well as other schools to a lesser extent, now work at Sayre through new and existing courses, internships, and research projects. As an outcome of the integration of health promotion and service activities in the curriculum, Sayre students act as *agents* of healthcare change in the Sayre neighborhood.

While the Health Promotion and Disease Prevention Program at Sayre was being planned, the School District of Philadelphia announced that it would convert this middle school (grades 6–8) to a high school (grades 9–12), the process to be completed in 2006–2007. This transformation includes focusing the overall curriculum on community health promotion. In this curriculum, health promotion activities are integrated with core-subject learning in science, social studies, math, and language arts, as well as in health, career education, and other classes. Ultimately, every curriculum unit will have a community education and/or community problem-solving component. (Usually this will function as the organizing theme of the unit.) Given this approach, Sayre students are not passive recipients of health information. Instead, exemplifying democratic devolution in action, they are active deliverers of information and coordination, and creative providers of service.[7]

A considerable number and variety of Penn academically based community service courses provide the resources and support that make it possible to operate, sustain, and develop the Sayre Health Promotion and Disease Prevention Program. Literally hundreds of Penn students (professional, graduate, and undergraduate) and some twenty faculty members, from a wide range of Penn schools and departments, work at Sayre. Since they are performing community service while engaged in academic research, teaching, and learning, they are simultaneously practicing their specialized skills and developing their moral and civic consciousness and democratic character. And since they are engaged in a highly integrated common project, they are also learning how to communicate, interact, and collaborate with each other in wholly unprecedented ways, which have measurably broadened their academic horizons.

In the spring of 2004, the Sayre Health Promotion and Disease Prevention Program established a community board to apply to the U.S. Department of Health and Human Services for funding to create a federally qualified health center. The application was successful, and the Sayre health clinic opened in 2006 to serve students, their families, and other community members.

The dean of Penn medicine, Arthur Rubenstein, recognized the extraordinary potential of the Sayre Health Promotion and Disease Prevention Program when he appointed Bernett L. Johnson, Jr., to the newly created position of senior associate dean for diversity and community outreach in the School of Medicine. Johnson, a distinguished professor of dermatology and the senior medical officer of the Hospital of the University of Pennsylvania, played the key role in engaging the medical school with the Sayre project, recruiting students, residents, house staff, and faculty to contribute to various health education and health promotion activities. In the announcement appointing Johnson, Dean Rubenstein wrote, "He will build upon our successful community efforts, many of which Dr. Johnson initiated, and work closely with colleagues at the university level to coordinate interactions with community groups and organizations."[8] It should be noted that Ira Harkavy had been advocating for such a position for nearly thirteen years. The Sayre Health Promotion and Disease Prevention Program provided the real-world demonstration necessary to convince the dean and other administrative leaders of the benefits that would accrue to both Penn medicine and West Philadelphia from creating an office designed to substantially increase and enhance the medical center's work with the community.

Though it is still in its early stages, we believe that the successful creation and operation of the Sayre Health Promotion and Disease Prevention Program strongly supports the validity of this basic proposition: universities can significantly help overcome the terribly harmful effects of disciplinary fragmentation and conflict, narrow specialization, bureaucratic barriers, and "ancient Customs and Habitudes" by identifying and actively trying to solve a highly complex, highly significant, real-world, *local community problem*, which, by its very nature, requires sustained interschool and interdisciplinary collaboration.

The Penn-Sayre project demonstrates that when universities such as Penn give very high priority to actively solving strategic, real-world, complex problems in their local communities, a much greater likelihood exists that they will significantly advance the public good. Moreover, it demonstrates that they also increase their capacity to translate the theoretical advantages of the "One University" idea into practical action, as well as help to create the university-assisted community schools that constitute highly strategic, practical means to help solve the Dewey Problem.

Democratic Partnerships and Communal
Participatory Action Research

Significant development of academically based community service-learning and research courses at Penn did not necessarily denote an ongoing *democratic* partnership with West Philadelphia schools and communities. The West Philadelphia Improvement Corps, now more widely known as the University-Assisted Community Schools Program, however, does provide the integrative, community-focused organizational vehicle that helps these courses make a vital difference in West Philadelphia schools and their communities.

Over time we have come to conceptualize the Center for Community Partnerships' work through WEPIC and university-assisted community schools as an ongoing communal participatory action research project designed to contribute simultaneously to the improvement of West Philadelphia and to Penn's relationship with West Philadelphia, as well as to the advancement of learning and knowledge. As an institutional strategy, communal participatory action research differs significantly from traditional action research. Both research processes are directed toward problems in the real world, are concerned with application, and are participatory, but they differ radically in the degrees to which they are continuous, comprehensive, and beneficial both to the organization or community studied and to the university.

For example, traditional action research is exemplified in the efforts developed by the late William Foote Whyte, Davydd Greenwood, and their associates at Cornell University in Ithaca, New York, to advance industrial democracy in the worker cooperatives of Mondragón, Spain.[9] Its considerable empirical and theoretical significance notwithstanding, the research at Mondragón is not at all an institutional necessity for Cornell. By contrast, the University of Pennsylvania's enlightened self-interest is directly tied to the success of its research efforts in West Philadelphia—hence its emphasis on, and continuing support for, communal participatory action research. In short, proximity to an easily accessible, inexpensive, "natural laboratory" and a focus on problems that are institutionally significant to the university encourage sustained, continuous research involvement. Put another way, *strategic community problem-solving research tends strongly to develop sustained, continuous research partnerships between a university and its local community.*

Given its fundamental democratic orientation, the center's participatory action research project has worked toward higher levels of participation by community members in problem identification and planning, as well as in implementation. To put it very euphemistically, this has not been easy to do. Based on decades of Penn's destructive action and inaction involving the local community, university-community conflicts take significant effort and time to reduce.[10] The center's work with university-assisted community schools has focused on health and nutrition, the environment, conflict resolution and peer mediation, community performance and visual arts, school and community publications, technology, school-to-career programs, and reading improvement. Each of these projects almost inevitably varies in the extent to which it engages and empowers public school students, teachers, parents, and other community members *in each stage of the research process.* Though it has a long way to go before it actually achieves its goal, the center's overall effort, however, has been *consciously* democratic and participatory—to genuinely work *with* the community, not *on* or *in* the community.

As university-assisted community schools and related projects have grown and developed, and as concrete positive outcomes for schools and neighborhoods have continued to occur (e.g., the Sayre healthcare center), community trust and participation have increased. It would be terribly misleading, however, if we left our readers with the impression that town-gown collaboration has completely—or even largely—replaced the town-gown conflicts that strongly characterized Penn-community relationships before 1985; it has not.

Penn is a leading American research university. Given the ferociously competitive nature of the American academic system, particularly as it developed after 1945, Penn feels compelled to compete ferociously with its rivals. As a result, it inevitably subjects itself to all of the pressures entailed by academic competition. Stated in propositional form, our basic argument can be summarized as follows:

competition among American universities tends strongly to produce university-community conflict.

That proposition's validity is virtually self-evident. Granted its validity, it seems understandable, even predictable, that to compete with their rivals in other universities, Penn administrators and faculty members frequently feel forced to adopt authoritative roles and to pursue policies that either result in serious conflicts with West Philadelphia residents, such as arrogantly invoking their "academic expertise" and sacrificing democratic processes to achieve short-term university development goals; or sharply distance Penn from concern with serious problems that West Philadelphia residents have had to confront since the end of World War II.

Since 1985, Penn's engagement with West Philadelphia schools and neighborhoods has come a long way. But Penn still has a very far distance to travel before it radically changes its hierarchical culture and structure and really uses its enormous resources to help transform West Philadelphia into a democratic, cosmopolitan, neighborly community and multidimensional asset for a major university. We do not intend to give the impression that we think we have largely solved the problem of developing *and implementing* the practical means needed to realize Dewey's theory of participatory democracy. We are well aware that we are a long way from having done so.

Having candidly acknowledged this reality, we think we have shown that a reasonable basis exists for the following proposition: if Penn (like all American research universities, an internally conflictual, highly complex, highly fragmented, corporate enterprise) ever does systematically decide to fully mobilize and integrate its enormous resources to help West Philadelphia transform itself into a Deweyan democratic, cosmopolitan, neighborly community, its best strategy would be to make optimum development of university-assisted community schools a very high institutional priority. We further believe that there is a real possibility that Penn will eventually commit itself to such a radical goal. To suggest why our optimism does not self-evidently convict us of delusionary utopianism, we begin by citing President Rodin's remarkable speech at an interfaith program honoring Martin Luther King, Jr.

President Judith Rodin's Inspiring Vision of Penn and West Philadelphia as Constituting a "Beloved Community"

On January 20, 2000, Penn held an "Interfaith Program" in honor of Martin Luther King, Jr. As part of that program, President Rodin presented Ira Harkavy with "the faculty award for bringing academically based service learning into reality." We cite that award in part because it testifies to the importance Penn gives to action-oriented, community problem-solving teaching and research. Far more significantly, however, Rodin chose that occasion to deliver an extraordinarily visionary speech, "Martin Luther King's Challenge: Service to Society." That speech represented by far the strongest statement she, or any senior Penn official, had made to support the idea that the "University and the City . . . stand on common ground, our futures very much intertwined."[11]

> More than 30 years after his earthly journey ended in Memphis, the Reverend Dr. Martin Luther King, Jr. remains a part of the light by which we chart our ongoing struggle for justice and human dignity for all. . . . Dr. King never stopped witnessing for justice. He never stopped working to create what he called a "beloved community."
>
> I am sure that were he with us today, Dr. King would compliment universities like Penn for producing brilliant, imaginative doctors, lawyers, scholars and scientists who push the envelopes of their disciplines and professions. He would commend us for conducting research that yields important advances in the health sciences and other fields. But he would also say that it is not enough. It is not enough to expand the intellect and talents of our students if we fail to rouse their souls to serve others and engage them in the larger issues of the day. Nor is it enough, he would say, for us to make great discoveries in the lab and develop theoretical solutions to society's problems if we do not use them to tackle the kinds of challenges we face every day. Dr. King would be right. But

I also believe he would be right at home at Penn, whose
founder professed a similar philosophy of education that
today guides us more than ever.

Dr. Franklin declared that "the great aim and end of all
learning is service to society." For Penn, society begins right
here in West Philadelphia—right here in this beloved community that we are building together.

During his life, Martin Luther King, Jr., was a supreme
challenger. He challenged the nation to change unjust laws.
He challenged a U.S. president to forsake war, and he challenged each of us to love and serve humanity as best we can.

By meeting Dr. King's challenge and rallying to his call,
each of us can help make Penn *the* [original emphasis]
national model for building a beloved community.[12]

We would be less than candid if we failed to observe that Rodin,
of course, knew that on January 20, 2000, Penn and West
Philadelphia did not really constitute anything like Dr. King's
"beloved community." The purpose of visionary speeches is not to
describe present reality, but rather to inspire people to change present reality for the better. Rodin's challenging speech eloquently envisioned a future day when university-community conflict would be
overcome and the Penn-West Philadelphia relationship would
indeed constitute something like "a beloved community."

President Amy Gutmann Proclaims a "Penn Compact" to "Serve Humanity and Society"

Having been president for ten years and significantly increased
Penn's commitment to engagement with its local community, Rodin
retired in 2004. She was succeeded by Amy Gutmann, a highly distinguished political philosopher whose scholarly work focused on the
role universities can play in advancing democratic education and
democratic societies. Logically enough, in her inaugural address on
October 15, 2004, President Gutmann emphasized that Penn was not

"an ivory tower" and proclaimed a remarkably comprehensive "Penn Compact" designed to fulfill the responsibility that universities have "to serve humanity and society." Among other far-reaching observations, she noted that,

> Through our collaborative engagement with communities all over the world, Penn is poised—and I think uniquely poised—to advance the central values of democracy in a great urban city: life, liberty, opportunity, and mutual respect.
>
> Effective engagement of these values, begins right here at home. We cherish our relations with our neighbors, relationships that have strengthened Penn academically and they have strengthened the vitality of West Philadelphia.

But the Penn Compact, Gutmann emphasized, will not be limited to West Philadelphia; it will "engage [the university] locally and globally."

> We will help drive economic development throughout the City and the Commonwealth. And we will build our national and international leadership by sharing the fruits of our knowledge both throughout our country and world. . . . By putting our principles into ever better practice, our Penn family will rise from excellence to eminence in our teaching and research.[13]

Both Gutmann's inaugural speech and Rodin's "beloved community" speech eloquently demonstrate that the idea of the "engaged, democratic, cosmopolitan, civic university" is alive and flourishing at Penn (as well as at many other American universities). Both speeches reinforce our conviction that to realize the idea of the truly engaged university, American academics must be powerfully moved into radical action by an inspiring vision of what American universities and American society can and should be. To suggest why such radical academic action is not an "impossible dream," in Chapter 7 we sketch the

accelerating progress of the University Civic Responsibility movement (our term for this development) in the United States, as well as
in a variety of countries throughout the world, and how that progress
might contribute to the eventual realization of Dewey's utopian vision
of an integrated worldwide "Great Community" of truly collaborative
and democratic societies.

7 The University Civic Responsibility Idea Becomes an International Movement

> *As the progress of learning consists not a little in the wise ordering and institutions of each university, so it would be yet much more advanced if there were a closer connection and relationship between all the different universities of Europe than now there is. . . . And surely as nature creates brotherhood in families, and arts mechanical contract brotherhood in societies, and the anointment of God superinduces a brotherhood in kings and bishops, and vows and regulations make a brotherhood in religious orders; so in like manner there cannot but be a noble and generous brotherhood contracted among men by learning and illumination, seeing that God himself is called "the Father of Lights."*
>
> FRANCIS BACON, THE ADVANCEMENT OF LEARNING (1605)

THE ACCELERATING POSITIVE CHANGES in Penn's relationship to its local schools and community are neither atypical nor unique to Penn. More or less similar changes taking place throughout the United States testify to the emergence of a University Civic Responsibility movement—a national movement to construct an organizationally integrated, optimally democratic schooling system, as the most strategic means to advance American democracy.

A convenient way to suggest the rapid development of that movement during the 1990s and early 2000s is to contrast its relatively flourishing condition today with the devastating indictment against American universities that Derek Bok, the president of Harvard University, presented in 1990. In a major book published that year,

President Bok strongly indicted American universities for failing to do what they should have been doing "to help our country cope more effectively with a formidable array of problems."[1] Less than a decade later, however, that condition had changed significantly for the better.

A national conference on Higher Education and Civic Responsibility was held June 18–20, 1998, in Tallahassee, Florida. Cosponsored by the American Council on Education and Florida State University, the conference brought together leaders from a wide variety of higher education institutions. The conference had two primary purposes:

> First, to set the agenda for a new National Forum on Higher Education and Civic Responsibility being initiated by the American Council on Education; and second, to survey the higher education landscape for the best programs involving civic responsibility. The Forum's goals will be to strengthen higher education's civic role both in educating students and institutional service to communities.[2]

The conference was a great success. To build on its success and help develop a coordinated national movement to increase the number of colleges and universities working to interactively improve the quality of life in their local communities and the moral and civic education of their students, the American Council on Education published a book of essays on *Civic Responsibility and Higher Education*.[3] Its publication in 2000 constituted a "hard" indicator of the accelerating growth and development of the idea that universities (i.e., all institutions of higher education) powerfully advance knowledge and learning when they take significant responsibility for the well-being of the local communities in which they constitute highly strategic corporate citizens.

In the preface to *Civic Responsibility and Higher Education*, its editor, Thomas Ehrlich, observes that it focuses on two central questions: (1) What does civic engagement mean? (2) What can colleges and universities do to promote it? Having posed these questions, Ehrlich summarizes the volume's contents as follows:

The essays in this volume should be of significant interest to everyone troubled about American democracy and its future, as well as about the future of higher education in this country. The authors have written with particular attention to college and university faculty and administrators and what they can do to educate their own students to be responsible citizens. No less important, these essays provide important insights on *how campuses themselves can be engaged citizens of their communities* [emphasis added]. But the volume is also written for a larger audience of those concerned about how to reverse the decline of civic engagement in the United States. The authors not only diagnose the reasons why higher education has been primarily on the sidelines during this decline, but also propose concrete steps to change that reality.[4]

As this summary suggests, the volume focuses on what "engaged" colleges and universities can do to promote democratic citizenship in America and how they can best function as "engaged citizens of their communities." *Civic Responsibility and Higher Education* received highly favorable reviews and significantly accelerated the progress of the nationwide movement for academic civic engagement. In fact, the movement progressed so rapidly that a national academic organization, the American Association for Higher Education, devoted its entire annual conference in 2002 to the theme "Knowledge for What? The Engaged Scholar." Simply listing some of the conference's "organizing emphasis areas" suggests the extent to which American higher eds now are engaging themselves with the problems of their local communities: "The Scholarship of Engagement"; "The Engaged Learner"; "The Faculty Role in Community Partnerships"; "Community-Based Research"; and "Laying the Foundations for a Democratic Society."

This chapter centers on developments relating to the past, present, and possible future of the American higher education system. It seems instructive—and inspiring—however, to place those developments in a broader context.

An International Academic Consortium
for the Advancement of Democracy

Characterized by the *New York Times* as a "Vast Rally for Democracy," a significant international conference was held June 26–27, 2002, in Warsaw, Poland. As though to dramatically symbolize the progress human beings have made in their long march toward global democracy and to John Dewey's "Great Community," the high-ranking delegates from over one hundred nations met "in the splendor of . . . [Warsaw's] ancient royal castle" to work "Toward a Community of Democracies."

According to the *Times*'s account, the conference organizers aimed to "encourage deeper democracy in the world by having countries commit themselves to what is being called the Warsaw Declaration." Hoping to "gain the currency of the Helsinki Declaration of 1975," the organizers chose that title to advance the movement for "deeper democracy" in the world, as the Helsinki Declaration had advanced the movement for "human rights."[5] It seems reasonable to predict that the Warsaw Declaration eventually will be viewed as a major turning point in the historic movement for global democracy. Whether or not that prediction turns out to be accurate, it is indisputable that universities throughout the world are increasingly participating in the emerging movement and collectively constitute one of its most strategic components.

Since we are university professors, our observation may seem self-serving or self-congratulatory. Its main purpose, however, is to highlight the significance of the truly unprecedented International Consortium for Higher Education, Civic Responsibility, and Democracy, which was formed in Strasbourg, France in 1999, even before the Warsaw Declaration was proclaimed. Convinced that "institutions of higher education can potentially function as strategic institutions in democratic political development," the consortium aims to increase their collective capacity to play that role far more effectively than they possibly could have if they acted alone. The consortium can be briefly described as a joint effort of the Council of Europe and the following U.S. higher educational associations represented on the U.S. steering committee of the consortium: American Association of Colleges and Universities, American Council on Education, and Campus Compact.[6]

To get its collective work under way, the consortium decided to undertake a highly ambitious, consciousness-raising, data-gathering, international research project on "Universities as Sites of Citizenship and Civic Responsibility."[7] The Council of Europe's Committee on Higher Education and Research functions as the administrative and operational center of activity for the European component of the project. It seems appropriate to note that the University of Pennsylvania functions as the organizational center for the American component, as well as for the research project and the international consortium as a whole.

Described somewhat more specifically, the project focuses on institutions of higher education as strategic institutions in democratic political and social development. It is conceived as a cross-national study comparing universities in over forty European countries, both new and established democracies, and in the fifty states of the United States. It assesses the actual activities of institutions of higher education that support democratic values and practices, and promotes the dissemination of those activities to increase the contributions of higher education to democracy on campus and in the local community and wider society.

The project is divided into three phases: (1) a pilot study of students, faculty, and administrators and their relationship to local governments, schools, businesses, and media and civic groups; (2) a survey of the above in a sample of approximately 125 institutions in Europe and a similar number in the United States; and (3) an analysis, formulation of recommendations, and distribution of materials that can be used by institutions of higher education to discuss and decide their responsibilities for civic education and democracy.

The primary purpose of the first phase, a pilot study, was to design a much larger cross-national comparative research project of universities and colleges as socializing *agents for democratic values and practices among their students and their local communities.* The objective was to map the variety of activities carved out by universities and colleges and to test selected instruments for assessing what is being done and to what effect. The U.S. pilot project was largely funded by the National Science Foundation; the European pilot project was supported by the Council of Europe. Now that the pilot study has been successfully completed, funds are being sought to conduct the far more expensive second and third phases of the project. When completed, this will be the first trans-Atlantic empirical study of its kind.

General academic contributions will include a systemic examination of arguably the core institution shaping democratic development; an empirical basis for developing theories of democratic development in the global era; instruments for assessing, understanding, and increasing the levels of civic responsibility in different societies; and an analysis to better understand the relationships among higher education, democratic schooling, and democratic societies. A by-product of this research will be the development of approaches, methodologies, and networks for intensive, multisite, comparative international study on a range of issues (e.g., health, culture, political socialization, and economic development). As evidence of progress, it is worth noting that the consortium has recently expanded its membership to include Australia, South Africa, and South Korea, and it is exploring expansion to countries in Asia and Latin America. In fact, in May 2005, Ira Harkavy spoke to a meeting of Uruguayan university leaders and senior governmental officials in Montevideo, Uruguay to introduce them to the international consortium. At the conclusion of the meeting, it was agreed to begin discussions designed to result in a national coalition of universities that would join the consortium, as well as to work with university leadership across southern Latin America (Argentina, Chile, Brazil, and Paraguay) to form a regional association dedicated to university engagement and education for democratic citizenship.

The meeting in Uruguay proved to be particularly well timed. A week before, members of the consortium's U.S. steering committee, co-chaired by Ira Harkavy, met with colleagues from the Council of Europe who have taken a leading role in the international consortium. Among other items discussed were the results of the pilot study,

"Universities as Sites of Citizenship and Civic Responsibility," as well as the activities of the Council's 2005 European Year of Citizenship through Education. Most important, a decision was made to significantly expand the number of nations in the consortium and to consider holding a global forum on higher education, democratic citizenship, and human rights at the Council of Europe headquarters in Strasbourg in June 2006.

In December 2005, at a meeting of the Council of Europe's Steering Committee for Higher Education and Research (CDESR), which was attended by members of the U.S. steering committee, agreement was reached to hold a Global Forum on the Responsibility of Higher Education for Democratic Culture, Citizenship, Human Rights, and Sustainability. In announcing the forum, the Council of Europe and the consortium leaders highlighted higher education's crucial role in the development of democratic education and societies:

> Along with the global spread of democratic ideas and societies, a crisis of commitment to and practice of democracy persists. Democracy cannot exist without strong institutions and sound legislation, but it also cannot work without being based on democratic culture. *Education and schooling are decisive forces shaping the democratic development of societies; and universities, in turn, are strategic institutions for the democratic development of schooling and societies* [emphasis added].
>
> A democratic culture encompasses democratic values, ways of knowing and acting, ethical judgments, analytical competencies, and skills of engagement. It includes concern for the sustainable well being of fellow human beings as well as of the environment in which we live. It includes awareness of and concern for human rights as well as openness to the cultural diversity of human experience and willingness to give due consideration to the views of others.
>
> *Higher education cannot remain indifferent to this challenge* [emphasis added].[8]

The global forum was held on June 22–23 in Strasbourg with approximately one hundred fifty educational leaders (including thirty-seven college and university presidents from the United States) and policymakers from around the world attending. A declaration was adopted by acclamation that calls for an increased commitment of higher education to democratic culture and for "higher education leaders and policy makers" to put the "values of democracy, human rights and social, environmental and economic sustainability" into practice through "action in their local as well as in the national and global communities."[9] The Council of Europe also agreed to host a Web site through which colleges and universities can sign the declaration and join a global network. An international conference to assess the progress of the network and propose future action will be held at Penn on March 29–30, 2007.

In our judgment, the International Consortium for Higher Education, Civic Responsibility, and Democracy will provide the organizational mechanism needed to help create an international network of academics who are dedicated to developing the practical means to realize Dewey's inspiring vision of a global "Great Community." When we view the formation of the consortium in historical perspective, its true significance is better appreciated. Viewed in historical perspective, we believe it potentially constitutes a major development in the progress of the Scientific Revolution, which Francis Bacon worked so hard to promote in the early seventeenth century.

Heated controversy continues to exist about Bacon's contributions to modern science and modern philosophy of science. Almost everyone agrees, however, that his eloquent, passionate prophecy of the great good that would result from development of a highly collaborative, genuinely experimental, science of inquiry powerfully contributed to the Scientific Revolution and the idea of progress it helped inspire and spread. To John Dewey, Bacon ranked as one of the great figures in world intellectual history.

In his major book entitled *Reconstruction in Philosophy*, Dewey hailed Bacon as "the great forerunner of the spirit of modern man," the "prophet of new tendencies," and the "real founder of modern thought." Bacon's devastating criticisms of the "great body of learning"[10] and aristocratic idealist theories and methodology handed down from antiquity, as well as his devastating criticisms of the quarrelsome, parochial, tradition-bound universities, which transmitted and perpetuated antiquated learning and methodology, Dewey observed, powerfully helped revolutionize scientific inquiry and effectively began modern thought. Among the major "defects" Bacon attributed to universities, their internal divisions and the failure of "all the different universities of Europe" to collaborate closely were highly ranked. Viewed from that perspective, the formation of the international consortium in 1999 can be characterized as a historic, positive organizational response to Bacon's critique of universities in his 1605 work *The Advancement of Learning*. The following is Bacon's most relevant passage:

> As the progress of learning consists not a little in the wise ordering and institutions of each university, so it would be yet much more advanced *if there were a closer connection and relationship between all the different universities of Europe than now there is* [emphasis added]. For we see there are many orders and societies which, though they be divided under distant sovereignties and territories, yet enter into and maintain among themselves a kind of contract and fraternity, in so much that they have governors (both provincial and general) whom they all obey. And surely as nature creates brotherhood in families, and arts mechanical contract brotherhood in societies, and the anointment of God superinduces a brotherhood in kings and bishops, and vows and regulations make a brotherhood in religious orders; so in like manner there cannot but be a noble and generous brotherhood contracted among men by learning and illumination, seeing that God himself is called "the Father of Lights."[11]

We have sketched the "big picture" of the new role universities are now beginning to play in the global movement for the integrated advancement of learning and democracy, so it seems appropriate to conclude this book with how we might progress beyond John Dewey by reporting on the present flourishing state of the revived movement for community schools in the United States. Among other reasons, it seems appropriate to do so because the relationships between American universities and community schools are now being closely studied by universities throughout the world for possible adaptation in their own countries and because we view the development of university-assisted community schools as the best strategy yet devised to solve the Dewey Problem, on which this book aims to stimulate serious, sustained, successful work.

8 John Dewey, the Coalition for Community Schools, and Developing a Participatory Democratic American Society

The Philosophers have only interpreted the world, in various ways; the point is to change it.

KARL MARX, *THESES ON FEUERBACH* (1845–1846)

I define wisdom as the application of intelligence and experience toward the attainment of a common good. . . . Wisdom might bring us a world that would seek . . . to better itself and the conditions of all the people in it. At some level, we as a society have a choice. What do we wish to maximize through our schooling? Is it just knowledge? Is it just intelligence? Or is it also wisdom? If it is wisdom, then we need to put our students on a much different course. We need to value not only how they use their outstanding individual abilities to maximize their attainments but how they use their individual abilities to maximize the attainments of others as well. We need, in short, to value wisdom. And then we need to remember that wisdom is not just about what we think, but more importantly how we act.

ROBERT J. STERNBERG, "FOUR ALTERNATIVE FUTURES FOR EDUCATION IN THE UNITED STATES: IT'S OUR CHOICE" (2004)

A S NOTED IN PREVIOUS CHAPTERS, during the twentieth century a variety of "movements" for community schools episodically rose and fell in the United States. Beginning in the mid-1980s, a powerful revival was under way, and efforts to link schools and communities grew exponentially. Since then, universities (e.g., Penn), local and state governments, the United Way, parent and neighborhood associations, and business, civic, religious, and social organizations have all become increasingly involved with schools and have creatively developed a variety of ways to make their efforts more effective. Though American communities vary widely, the common goal has been to create support systems that help to improve learning, as well as a variety of related outcomes for children and youth, family members, and community residents "of all ages and classes" (the phrase Dewey used in 1902 to advocate his greatly expanded conception of neighborhood school functions).

As linkages between schools and other community institutions grew exponentially throughout the United States during the 1990s, the need to create some central information and coordinating agency became increasingly obvious. Early in 1997, therefore, community and school leaders began a series of meetings to discuss the problem. So much progress was made that the Emerging Coalition for Community Schools was formed in October 1997. The name was deliberately chosen to suggest the highly diverse membership, open-minded, flexible nature of the coalition and the wide variation in the community school models then being developed throughout the country.

To get the work of the coalition effectively under way, Michael Usdan, the president of the Institute for Educational Leadership, agreed to provide office space at the institute's long-established, centrally located headquarters in Washington, DC, and to have Martin Blank, who was then staffing the Institute's school and community work, provide staff support for the coalition. As evidence that the community school idea was "an idea whose time had again come," a planning grant was quickly secured for the coalition. Generous grants soon followed from leading foundations concerned with school and/or community development. Given the coalition's rapid expansion of membership and activities, "Emerging" was soon dropped from its name.[1]

Testifying to the coalition's remarkable growth, its "partners" (i.e., members) now include more than 165 leading local, state, and national organizations (e.g., Chicago Public Schools, National Governors' Association, American Federation of Teachers, Carnegie

Corporation, Charles Stewart Mott Foundation, Children's Defense Fund, United Way of America) and its work is overseen by a broadly based steering committee. To avoid misunderstanding—since Ira Harkavy has served as chairperson of the coalition from the start of operations and in his own work focuses on developing the university-assisted community school model—we think it best to emphasize explicitly that the coalition supports development of many different community school models and encourages communities to choose the one most appropriate for their particular needs, resources, and histories. To clarify and amplify that critical point, the following quotation is from *Community Schools: Partnerships for Excellence*, a brochure that the coalition uses to define and advertise itself. The brochure's cover proclaims that its mission is "Strengthening Schools, Families, and Communities" and emphasizes that

> [a] community school is both a set of partnerships and a place where services, supports, and opportunities lead to improved student learning, stronger families, and healthier communities. *Using public schools as a hub* [emphasis added], inventive, enduring relationships among educators, families, community volunteers, business, health and social service agencies, youth development organizations, and others committed to children are changing the educational landscape—permanently—by transforming traditional schools into partnerships for excellence.[2]

The coalition's brochure does not explicitly invoke John Dewey's theories of community schools, experimental instrumentalism, and participatory democracy, but as the following epigraph from the brochure suggests, a Deweyan perspective imbues the coalition's basic philosophy:

> The community schools, whatever the differences among them caused by varying economic and social patterns, have a common philosophy. *These schools are based upon the*

*democratic ideal of respect for each individual person and his
[or her] right to participate in the affairs of the community
which concern the common good* [emphasis added]. . . . Such
a program is characterized by change in response to changing
needs, continuous experimentation to seek out satisfactory
ways of achieving common goals and careful evaluation of the
results of its activities.[3]

In Chapter 3, we expressed astonishment that Dewey failed to
use the community school idea that he had brilliantly advocated in
1902 to help solve the critical problem he raised (but evaded trying
to solve in 1927 in *The Public and its Problems*), namely, how democratic, cosmopolitan, neighborly communities could pragmatically be
constructed in the United States. That Dewey logically should have
used the community school idea to help achieve his end-in-view of
constructing a participatory democratic American society becomes
clear when we consider the far-reaching implications of another quotation from the coalition's brochure. After posing the question of
"what a community school looks like," the brochure then gives the
following quintessentially Dewey-Clapp-Seay answer:

A wide range of models and approaches can fit into a basic
community school framework. Every school is unique, but
here's the coalition's broad vision of a well-developed community school. A community school, operating in a public
school building, is open to students' families and the community before, during and after school, seven days a week,
all year long. It is operated jointly between the school system and one or more community agencies. Families, youth,
principals, teachers and neighborhood residents help design
and implement activities that promote high educational
achievement and *use the community as a resource for learning* [emphasis added].

The school is oriented toward the community, encourag-
ing student learning through community service and service

learning. A before-and-after school learning component allows students to build on their classroom experiences, expand their horizons, contribute to their communities and have fun. A family support center helps families with child-rearing, employment, housing and other services. Medical, dental, and mental health services are readily accessible. . . . Community schools open up new channels for learning and self expression. . . . To achieve their desired results, most community schools over time consciously link activities in the following areas: a quality education; positive youth development; family support; family and community engagement in decision making; and community development.[4]

Though Dewey passionately called for the construction of participatory democracy in *The Public and Its Problems*, he made no attempt to develop the community school idea that his book logically should have developed—and that the Coalition for Community Schools is now developing in real-world practice. The coalition's increasing impact is effectively illustrated by the Full Service Community Schools Act, introduced in the U.S. House of Representatives in June 2004 by Steny Hoyer, the House Democratic whip (at this writing, the presumptive House majority leader). The act authorizes funding for full-service community schools that coordinate multiple federal, state, and local educational and social service programs in partnership with school districts, community-based organizations, and public-private partnerships.[5] Members of the coalition, particularly Joy Dryfoos, the noted educational researcher and author, assisted the congressman and his staff in conceptualizing and drafting the bill. Representative Hoyer issued a media release announcing the act immediately following a meeting with the coalition's steering committee and leaders of major organizations active in the coalition.[6]

Among other reasons, we have cited the coalition's flourishing state and expanding activities, as well as the development of the numerous other organizational innovations sketched in previous chapters, to support this book's basic proposition:

The Dewey Problem *is* soluble *if* democratically minded academics throughout the world work continuously, *collaboratively*, and creatively to solve it. As our preface emphasizes, our primary purpose is *agenda-setting, movement-initiating,* not *particular thesis-proving.* To invoke Dewey's historical proposition, the world's "present situation with its problems"[7] makes it imperative that democratically minded academics now give extremely high priority to developing and *effectively implementing* the practical means required to realize John Dewey's utopian theory of participatory democracy in modern societies. Solving that critical problem, we contend, would significantly help bring about the worldwide "Great Community," which, as Dewey envisioned it, would at last enable all human beings to lead long, healthy, active, peaceful, virtuous, and happy lives. Convinced that Dewey was right, we conclude this book by proclaiming a challenging Democratic Manifesto:

Academics of the world unite! Help solve the Dewey Problem!

■■ Acknowledgments
■■

W E WISH TO ACKNOWLEDGE our gratitude to our school and community partners, as well as the staff of the Center for Community Partnerships, particularly its longstanding associate directors, Cory Bowman, Joann Weeks, and Winnie Smart Mapp. We also thank the organizations, foundations, and agencies that have supported various aspects of our research and practice to develop university-assisted community schools: Charles Stewart Mott Foundation, W. K. Kellogg Foundation, Jessie Ball duPont Fund, State Farm Insurance Corporation, Wallace Funds, Carnegie Corporation of New York, William Penn Foundation, W. T. Grant Foundation, Rockefeller Foundation, Spencer Foundation (which awarded a postdoctoral fellowship to John Puckett), National Institutes of Health, Lilly Foundation, National Science Foundation, Corporation for National and Community Service, U.S. Department of Housing and Urban Development, U.S. Department of Labor, U.S. Department of Education, Commonwealth of Pennsylvania Department of Labor and Industry, Commonwealth of Pennsylvania Department of Education, Philadelphia Department of Health, and the members of the national advisory board of the Center for Community Partnerships.

To cite all of the other friends, colleagues, critics, students, and libraries who have contributed to our knowledge and enlightenment while we worked on this book would require too lengthy a list to be recalled accurately and printed here. We would be remiss, however, if we failed to note explicitly that we have learned—and continue to learn—a great deal from Robert Westbrook's critically important book *John Dewey and American Democracy*, and from continuing conversations with him. Among other things, he has helped us to see that solving the Dewey Problem should constitute an extremely high—arguably the highest—priority for democratically minded academics throughout the world in the twenty-first century.

PHILADELPHIA, PENNSYLVANIA
DECEMBER 2006

▪▪ Authorship

W E WISH TO NOTE that our authorship of this book has been a genuine collaboration—one that evolved over the course of innumerable conversations and debates among the three of us. It is no exaggeration to say that each of us has served as the others' research assistant and bibliographer.

Notes

INTRODUCTION

1. John Dewey, "Ethics of Democracy," in *The Early Works of John Dewey, 1882–1888*, vol. 1, ed. Jo Ann Boydston (Carbondale: Southern Illinois University, 1969), 237. Quotations from *Early Works* were verified in Larry Hickman, ed., *The Collected Works of John Dewey, 1882–1953: The Electronic Edition* (Charlottesville, VA: InteLex Corporation, 1996).

2. Robert Westbrook, *John Dewey and American Democracy* (Ithaca, NY: Cornell University Press, 1991), xiv–xv. It seems worth noting that Dewey himself never used the specific term "participatory democracy" to characterize his general theory of democracy. That term, however, is highly appropriate because it neatly catches the participatory essence of Dewey's comprehensive theory, which emphasizes that democracy is much more than a form of government; it is a "way of life" in which all citizens actively, and appropriately, participate in making and implementing all the communal, societal, and institutional decisions that significantly shape their lives. We were indeed surprised to discover that Dewey never actually used the term that has been frequently used to characterize his democratic theory and is now commonly used by people who know little, if anything, about its Deweyan inspiration. We discovered this when we made an electronic keyword search of all of Dewey's published works in Hickman, *Electronic Edition*.

General agreement now exists that the specific term "participatory democracy" was coined in 1960 by Arnold Kaufman, a philosopher at the University of Michigan. It was then popularized in 1962 by Tom Hayden, one of his students, in the extraordinarily influential *Port Huron Statement* of the radical student movement Students for a Democratic Society. For a succinct account of the term's coinage and Deweyan inspiration, see the brilliant review essay on the history of the general theory of participatory democracy by Jane Mansbridge, "On the Idea

That Participation Makes Better Citizens," in *Citizen Competence and Democratic Institutions*, ed. Stephen L. Elkin and Karol Edward Soltan (University Park: Pennsylvania State University Press, 1999), 311–15. Dewey, of course, was only one of a number of theorists who, for a variety of reasons, strongly advocated some form of participatory democracy.

CHAPTER 1

1. Robert Westbrook, *John Dewey and American Democracy* (Ithaca, NY: Cornell University Press, 1991), 13–38; the quotation is from 37–38. See also Neil Coughlan, *Young John Dewey* (Chicago: University of Chicago Press, 1975), 54–93.

2. Westbrook, *John Dewey*, 37–38.

3. Ibid., 38–43.

4. John Dewey, "The Ethics of Democracy," in *The Early Works of John Dewey, 1882–1888*, vol. 1, ed. Jo Ann Boydston (Carbondale: Southern Illinois University Press, 1969), 237–38. Quotations for *Early Works* were verified in Larry Hickman, ed., *The Collected Works of John Dewey, 1882–1953: The Electronic Edition* (Charlottesville, VA: InteLex Corporation, 1996).

5. Ibid., 239–40.

6. Ibid., 245–46.

7. Ibid., 246.

8. Westbrook, *John Dewey*, 48–51.

9. Ibid., 51; Westbrook quotes from John Dewey, "The Scholastic and the Speculator," *Early Works*, vol. 3.

10. Ibid., 52–58.

11. Ibid., 52–53.

12. Dewey quoted in Coughlan, *Young John Dewey*, 97.

13. Coughlan, *Young John Dewey*, 93–98. The quotation in the text is from 97–98.

14. Ibid., 98–99.

15. Ibid., 100–101.

16. Ibid., 101–2.

17. Ibid., 102–6.

18. Ibid., 96.

19. Westbrook, *John Dewey*, 55–58.

20. Ellen Condliffe Lagemann, "Experimenting with Education," in *Feminist Interpretations of John Dewey*, ed. Charlene Haddock Seigfried (University Park: Pennsylvania State University Press, 2002), 32.

CHAPTER 2

1. Wayne A. R. Leys, introduction to *The Early Works of John Dewey, 1893–1894*, vol. 4, ed. Jo Ann Boydston (Carbondale: Southern Illinois University Press, 1969), xvi–xvii. Quotations from *Early Works* were verified in Larry Hickman, ed., *The Collected Works of John Dewey, 1882–1953: The Electronic Edition* (Charlottesville, VA: InteLex Corporation, 1996).

2. Woodie Thomas White, "The Study of Education at the University of Chicago: 1892–1958" (unpublished PhD dissertation, University of Chicago, 1977), 11–24; quotations from pp. 13, 24. This dissertation is a valuable source of information and insights about Harper's creation of the Department of Pedagogy, accelerating interest in public schools, and changing views on the importance of the academic study of education to the University of Chicago.

3. Ibid., 24–28. White provides valuable quotations from the correspondence between Harper and Bulkley while she was in Europe.

4. Tufts's letter to Harper is conveniently printed in William W. Brickman and Stanley Lehrer, eds., *John Dewey: Master Educator*, rev. ed. (New York: Atherton Press, 1965), 167–68. In that volume, however, Tufts's letter does not include the list of "more important publications of Professor Dewey." We found that list when we tracked down Tufts's original letter in the *Collection of President's Papers, 1889–1925*, in the Department of Special Collections, in the Joseph Regenstein Library of the University of Chicago. For a highly informative, insightful account of the relationship between Harper and Dewey at Chicago, see Robert L. McCaul, "Dewey, Harper, and the University of Chicago," in Brickman and Lehrer, eds., *John Dewey: Master Educator*, 31–92. See also the thoughtful account in Robert Westbrook, *John Dewey and American Democracy* (Ithaca, NY: Cornell University Press, 1991), 59–113, esp. p. 83, which emphasizes the impact on Dewey of the move from Ann Arbor to Chicago.

5. Westbrook, *John Dewey*, 83.

6. Robert McCaul, "Dewey's Chicago," *School Review* 69 (1959): 267, quoted in White, "Study of Education at University of Chicago," 15. For our views on the Harper-Dewey relationship at the University of Chicago, see Lee Benson and Ira Harkavy, "University-Assisted Community Schools as Democratic Public Works," *The Good Society* 9 (1999): 14–20; Benson and Harkavy, "Integrating the American System of Higher, Secondary, and Primary Education to Develop Civic Responsibility," in *Civic Responsibility and Higher Education*, ed. Thomas Ehrlich (Phoenix: Oryx, 2000), 174–96.

7. For Harper's view of the university as the "Messiah" of democracy, see his 1899 address "The University and Democracy," in William Rainey Harper, *The Trend in Higher Education* (Chicago: University of Chicago Press, 1905), 1–34. See also the highly insightful study of Harper and the University of Chicago by James P. Wind, *The Bible and the University: The Messianic Vision of William Rainey Harper* (Atlanta: Scholars Press, 1987).

8. Harper, "The University and Democracy," 32.

9. Ibid., 25.

10. Wind, *The Bible and the University*, 2–5.

11. Ibid., 4–5.

12. Harper, "The University and Democracy," 19.

13. Ibid., 21.

14. Ibid., 27–28.

15. Ibid., 19–20.

16. William Rainey Harper, "The Urban University," in Harper, *The Trend in Higher Education*, 158.

17. Ibid., 158–60.

18. Steven M. Cahn, introduction to *The Later Works of John Dewey, 1925-1953*, vol. 13, ed. Jo Ann Boydston (Carbondale: Southern Illinois University Press, 1981), xvi-xvii. Cahn quotes from Dewey's "The Determination of Ultimate Values or Aims through Antecedent or A Priori Speculation or through Pragmatic Inquiry," *Later Works*, vol. 13. Quotations from *Later Works* were verified in Hickman, *Electronic Edition*.

19. Ibid., xvii–xviii.

20. John Dewey, "Ethical Principles Underlying Education," in Boydston, *Early Works*, vol. 5, 54–83.

21. Ibid, 59.

22. Ibid., 59–63.

23. For an insightful analysis of the school, see Westbrook, *John Dewey*, 96–113.

24. John Dewey, *The School and Society*, in *The Middle Works of John Dewey, 1899–1924*, vol. 1, ed. Jo Ann Boydston (Carbondale: Southern Illinois University Press, 1978), 7–8. Quotations from *Middle Works* were verified in Larry Hickman, ed., *The Collected Works of John Dewey, 1882–1953: The Electronic Edition* (Charlottesville, VA: InteLex Corporation, 1996).

25. Ibid., 25.

26. Ibid., 9.

27. Ibid., 25.

28. Ibid., 23.

29. Ibid., 18.

30. For a detailed analysis of the extent to which Dewey was strongly influenced by Wundt, see the chapter on "Wundtian Voluntarism," in John R. Shook, *Dewey's Empirical Theory of Knowledge and Reality* (Nashville: Vanderbilt University Press, 2000), 71–120.

31. For a fuller, and much more detailed critique of Dewey's 1899 lectures on *School and Society* and the scientistic character of his laboratory school than is presented in this book, see Lee Benson and Ira Harkavy, "School and Community in the Global Society," *Universities and Community Schools* 5, nos. 1–2 (1997): 23–28.

32. Dewey, *The School and Society*, 12.

33. Ibid., 8.

34. See and cf. Philip Jackson's incisive critique of the Laboratory School in his introduction to the centennial edition of Dewey's *The School and Society* and *The Child and the Curriculum* (Chicago: University of Chicago Press, 1990), ix–xli, esp. xxix–xxxiii.

35. Westbrook, *John Dewey*, 97–101.

36. For a particularly insightful and persuasive analysis of the "contributions of Jane Addams and the women of the Hull House Settlement to pragmatist theory, particularly as formulated by John Dewey," see Charlene Haddock Seigfried, "Socializing Democracy: Jane Addams and John Dewey," *Philosophy of the Social Sciences* 29 (June 1999): 207–30. See also Ira Harkavy and John Puckett, "Lessons from Hull House for the Contemporary Urban University," *Social Service Review* 68, no. 3 (1994): 299–321.

37. John Dewey, "The School as Social Centre," in *The Middle Works of John Dewey, 1899–1924*, vol. 2, ed. Jo Ann Boydston (Carbondale: Southern Illinois University Press, 1978), 80–93.

38. Ibid., 80.

39. Ibid., 80–81.

40. Ibid., 82.

41. Ibid.

42. Ibid., 83.

43. Ibid., 83–84.

44 Ibid., 84–89.

45. Ibid., 89. Our insertion of "people" denotes our recognition that Dewey always wrote in the masculine case.

46. Ibid., 90.

47. Ibid.

48. Ibid., 90–92.

49. Ibid., 92–93.

50. For an insightful analysis of Bacon's conception of science, see Paolo Rossi, "Bacon's Idea of Science," in *The Cambridge Companion to Bacon*, ed. Markuu Peltonen (Cambridge: Cambridge University Press), 25–28.

51. Dewey, "The School as Social Centre," 90.

52. Ibid., 93.

53. Ibid., 82.

54. Ibid., 93.

55. Ibid., 90.

CHAPTER 3

1. For Dewey's quarrel with Harper and his departure for Columbia University, see the accounts in Robert L. McCaul, "Dewey, Harper, and the University of Chicago," in *John Dewey: Master Educator*, rev. ed., ed. William W. Brickman and Stanley Lehrer (New York: Atherton Press, 1965), 62–74; and Robert Westbrook, *John Dewey and American Democracy* (Ithaca: Cornell University Press, 1991), 111–13.

2. Westbrook, *John Dewey*, 113.

3. Harold Rugg, *Foundations for American Education* (Yonkers, NY: World Book Company, 1947), 554–55.

4. John Dewey, *Democracy and Education*, in *The Middle Works of John Dewey, 1899–1924*, vol. 9, ed. Jo Ann Boydston (Carbondale: Southern Illinois University Press, 1978), 6. Quotations from *Middle Works* were verified in Larry Hickman, ed., *The Collected Works of John Dewey, 1882–1953: The Electronic Edition* (Charlottesville, VA: InteLex Corporation, 1996).

5. Ibid., 7.

6. Ibid., 6.

7. Ibid., 7.

8. Ibid., 7–9.

9. Ibid., 11–13.

10. James Guinlock, introduction to *The Later Works of John Dewey, 1925–1953*, vol. 2, ed. Jo Ann Boydston (Carbondale: Southern Illinois University Press, 1981), xxiii–xxiv. Quotations from *Later Works* were verified in Hickman, *Electronic Edition.*

11. John Dewey, "Ethics of Democracy," in *The Early Works of John Dewey, 1882–1888*, vol. 1, ed. Jo Ann Boydston (Carbondale: Southern Illinois University, 1969), 246. Quotations from *Early Works* were verified in Hickman, *Electronic Edition.*

12. John Dewey, *The Public and Its Problems*, in Boydston, *Later Works*, vol. 2, 325–28.

13. Ibid., 367–68.

14. Ibid, 369.

15. Ibid., 368.

16. Ibid., 370.

17. Ibid., 371.

18. Ibid., 371–72.

19. Ibid., 333.

20. Ibid.

21 Ibid.

22. Westbrook, *John Dewey*, 317–18.

CHAPTER 4

1. For appraisals of Elsie Clapp and Arthurdale, see Stephen E. Haid, "Arthurdale: An Experiment in Community Planning, 1933–1947" (PhD diss., University of West Virginia, 1975); Blanche Wiesen Cook, *Eleanor Roosevelt*, vol. 2, 1933–1938 (New York: Viking, 1999); Sam F. Stack, Jr., *Elsie Ripley Clapp (1897–1965): Her Life and the Community School* (New York: Lang, 2004); Daniel Perlstein, "Community and Democracy in American Schools: Arthurdale and the Fate of Progressive Education," *Teachers College Record* 97, no. 4 (1996): 625–50; Michael C. Johanek and John L. Puckett, *Leonard Covello and the Making of Benjamin Franklin High School: Education as if Citizenship Mattered* (Philadelphia: Temple University Press, 2007).

2. Elsie R. Clapp, preface to *Community Schools in Action* (New York: Viking, 1939), v.

3. John Dewey, foreword to *Community Schools in Action*, vii.

4. Ibid., vii–viii.

5. Ibid., viii–ix.

6. Ibid., ix.

7. Ibid., x.

8. See cases in Johanek and Puckett, *Leonard Covello*, esp. Benjamin Franklin High School in East Harlem, New York City, chaps. 4–7.

9. Nelson B. Henry, ed., *Forty-Fourth Yearbook of the National Society for the Study of Education, Part I: Curriculum Reconstruction* (Chicago: University of Chicago Press, 1945), v.

10. Maurice F. Seay, "The Community School Emphasis in Postwar Education," in Henry, *Forty-Fourth Yearbook*, 209.

11. Ibid.

12. Ibid., 209–10.

13. Ibid., 226.

14. Ibid., 227

15. Nelson B. Henry, ed., *Fifty-Second Yearbook of the National Society for the Study of Education, Part II: The Community School* (Chicago: University of Chicago Press, 1953), vii.

16. Paul R. Hanna and Robert A. Naslund, "The Community School Defined," in Henry, *Fifty-Second Yearbook*, 52.

17. Maurice F. Seay and John H. Wilkinson, "Overcoming Barriers to the Development of Community Schools," in Henry, *Fifty-Second Yearbook*, 286–87.

18. Johanek and Puckett, *Leonard Covello*, chap. 8. Although support for community schools declined after 1953, it should be emphasized that the Charles Stewart Mott Foundation has actively supported community schools and community education from 1934 to the present.

CHAPTER 5

1. William Rainey Harper, "The University and Democracy," in Harper, *The Trend in Higher Education* (Chicago: University of Chicago Press, 1905), 12.

2. Donald Kennedy, *Academic Duty* (Cambridge, MA: Harvard University Press, 1997), 265–88, 299.

3. For a highly perceptive, devastatingly critical analysis of Bush's report, *Science and the Endless Frontier*, see Donald E. Stokes, *Pasteur's Quadrant: Basic Science and Technological Innovation* (Washington, DC: The Brookings Institution Press, 1997).

4. For an illuminating discussion of the American university's democratic mission, see Charles W. Anderson, *Prescribing the Life of the Mind* (Madison: University of Wisconsin Press, 1993); and Anderson, "Pragmatism, Idealism, and the Aims of Liberal Education," in *Education and Democracy*, ed. Robert Orrill (New York: College Board Publications, 1997), 111–30. See also Ira Harkavy, "School-Community-University Partnerships: Effectively Integrating Community Building and Education Reform," *Universities and Community Schools* 6, no. 1–2 (1999): 7–24.

5. Discussion of the concept of a democratic devolution revolution is found in testimony by Ira Harkavy before the Subcommittee on Housing and Community Opportunity of the Committee on Banking and Financial Services of the House of Representatives, 105 Cong. 1 sess. (Washington, DC: U.S. Government Printing Office, 1997).

6. John W. Gardner, "Remarks to the Campus Compact Strategic Planning Committee," San Francisco, February 10, 1998.

7. Ibid.

8. See Ernest L. Boyer, "Creating the New American College," *Chronicle of Higher Education*, March 9, 1994, p. A48; Derek C. Bok, *Universities and the*

Future of America (Durham, NC: Duke University Press, 1990), *passim*; Lee Schulman, "Professing the Liberal Arts," in Orrill, *Education and Democracy*, 151–73; Alexander W. Astin, "Liberal Education and Democracy: The Case for Pragmatism" in Orrill, *Education and Democracy*, 207–23.

9. William R. Greiner, "In the Total of All These Acts: How Can American Universities Address the Urban Agenda?" *Universities and Community Schools* 4, no. 1–2 (1994): 12.

10. For an illuminating discussion of the concept of organizational learning, see William F. Whyte, ed., *Participatory Action Research* (Newbury Park, CA: Sage, 1991), 237–41.

11. For more complete accounts of Professor Johnston's work, see Lee Benson and Ira Harkavy, "Anthropology 210, Academically Based Community Service and the Advancement of Knowledge, Teaching, and Learning: An Experiment in Progress," *Universities and Community Schools* 2, no. 1–2 (1994): 66–69; Ira Harkavy, Frank Johnston, and John L. Puckett, "The University of Pennsylvania's Center for Community Partnerships as an Organizational Innovation for Advancing Action Research," *Concepts and Transformation* 1, no. 1 (1996): 15–29; Frank Johnston, et al., "The Urban Nutrition Initiative: Bringing Academically Based Community Service to the University of Pennsylvania's Department of Anthropology," *Michigan Journal of Community Service Learning* 10, no. 3 (2004): 100–106.

12. A fuller definition of public interest anthropology can be found in Peggy Reeves Sanday's "Opening Statement: Defining Public Interest Anthropology," presented at Symposium on Defining Public Interest Anthropology, 97th Annual Meeting of the American Anthropological Association, Philadelphia, December 3, 1998. Available at http://www.sas.upenn.edu/~psanday/pia.99.html.

13. We define "strategic academically based community service" as service rooted in and intrinsically tied to teaching and research. It aims to bring about structural community improvement (e.g., effective public schools, neighborhood economic development, strong community organizations) rather than simply to alleviate individual misery (e.g., feeding the hungry, sheltering the homeless, tutoring the learning disabled).

CHAPTER 6

1. Provost's Council on Undergraduate Education, "The 21st Century Penn Undergraduate Experience: Phase I," University of Pennsylvania, *Almanac* 41, no. 33 (May 1995), S-1.

2. University of Pennsylvania, "Annual Report, 1994–1995" (President's report, Philadelphia, 1996).

3. Samuel H. Preston, "Dean's Column," *Penn Arts and Sciences*, Fall 1998, 2.

4. "Dancing in the Shadows," *Penn Arts and Sciences*, Fall 1998, 9.

5. The description of Imagining America is available at http://www.ia.umich.edu. Rebecca Bushnell's remarks are from her address "Making the Connection: Democracy, Cultural Partnerships, and the University," opening keynote to

Imagining America International Conference, University of Pennsylvania, Philadelphia, November 5, 2004.

6. See Meyer Reinhold, "Opponents of Classical Learning in America during the Revolutionary Period," *Proceedings of the American Philosophical Society* 112, no. 4 (1968): 224.

7. The collaborative initiative to establish the Health Promotion and Disease Prevention Program and its related curriculum project aligns with the concept of "public work citizenship" advanced by scholar-activist Harry C. Boyte of the Humphrey Institute. In public work, diverse groups work together across racial, economic, and other social boundaries to "build" solutions to problems of mutual concern. See Harry C. Boyte and Nancy N. Kari, *Building America: The Democratic Promise of Public Work* (Philadelphia: Temple University Press, 1994); Boyte, *Everyday Politics: Reconnecting Citizens and Public Life* (Philadelphia: University of Pennsylvania Press, 2004).

8. Arthur H. Rubenstein and Ralph W. Muller, personal communication, December 22, 2004.

9. William F. Whyte and Kathleen K. Whyte, *Making Mondragón: The Growth and Dynamics of the Worker Cooperative Complex* (Ithaca, NY: ILR Press, 1988); Davydd J. Greenwood and José Luis Gonzalez Santos, *Industrial Democracy as Process: Participatory Action Research in the Fagor Cooperative Group of Mondragón* (Assen/Maastricht: Van Gorcum, 1992).

10. Ira Harkavy and John L. Puckett, "The Role of Mediating Structures in University Community Revitalization: The University of Pennsylvania and West Philadelphia as a Case Study," *Journal of Research and Development in Education* 25, no. 1 (1991): 10–25.

11. Part of President Rodin's speech, "Martin Luther King's Challenge," was published in *Almanac* 46, no. 18 (January 25, 2000), 6. The *Almanac* is Penn's official magazine of record. The reference in our text to the "University and the City . . . stand on common ground" statement is from Penn's official *Annual Report for 1987–1988*. For the radical change that statement represented in Penn's relationship to West Philadelphia, see Benson and Harkavy, "Progressing beyond the Welfare State: A Neo-Deweyan Strategy," *Universities and Community Schools* 2 (1991): 13–14.

12. Rodin, "Martin Luther King's Challenge."

13. President Gutmann's speech, "A Penn Compact," was printed in *Almanac* 46, no. 18 (October 19, 2004): S6–7.

CHAPTER 7

1. Derek Bok, *Universities and the Future of America* (Durham, NC: Duke University Press, 1990). Bok's book and Ernest Boyer's *Scholarship Reconsidered: Profiles of the Professoriate* (Princeton, NJ: Carnegie Foundation for the Advancement of Teaching, 1990) are arguably the two works that most significantly contributed to the University Civic Responsibility Movement.

2. See our discussion of the conference in Benson and Harkavy, *Universities and Community Schools* 6 (1999): 3–4.

3. Thomas Ehrlich, ed., *Civic Responsibility and Higher Education* (Phoenix: Oryx, 2000).

4. Ibid., v–vi.

5. Jane Perlez, "Vast Rally for Democracy Opens in a Polish Castle," *New York Times*, June 26, 2000, A9.

6. Our description of the consortium and its work is taken from the document it widely circulated in 2000, *An Overview of the International Consortium on Higher Education, Civic Responsibility and Democracy and the "Universities as Sites of Citizenship and Civic Responsibility" Research Project*.

7. International Consortium for Higher Education, Civic Responsibility, and Democracy, "Pilot Study: Universities as Sites of Citizenship and Civic Responsibility," http://www.upenn.edu/ccp/programs/consortium/research.shtml. It should be noted that the Universities as Sites of Citizenship and Civic Responsibility project has resulted in a series of presentations, articles, book chapters, and monographs; for example, see Sjur Bergan, ed., *The University as Res Publica: Higher Education, Governance, Student Participation and the University as a Site of Citizenship* (Strasbourg, France: Council of Europe Publishing, 2004); Alexander Winter, John Wiseman, and Bruce Muirhead, *Beyond Rhetoric: University-Community Engagement in Victoria* (Brisbane, Australia: Eidos, 2005).

8. Council of Europe, "The Responsibility of Higher Education for a Democratic Culture," http://www.coe.int/T/DG4/HigherEducation/Democratic Culture/Default_EN.asp#TopOfPage

9. Council of Europe, "Declaration on the Responsibility of Higher Education for Democratic Culture," June 23, 2006, http://www.coe.int/T/DG4/Higher Education/DemocraticCulture/Declaration_EN.pdf. The declaration includes a call for a special effort on or around 10 December, which is the International Day of Human Rights and the time at which the Nobel Peace Prize is presented.

10. John Dewey, *Reconstruction in Philosophy*, in *The Middle Works of John Dewey, 1899–1924*, vol. 12, ed. Jo Ann Boydston (Carbondale: Southern Illinois University Press, 1978), 95. Originally published in 1920. Quotations from *Middle Works* were verified in Larry Hickman, ed., *The Collected Works of John Dewey, 1882–1953: The Electronic Edition* (Charlottesville, VA: InteLex Corporation, 1996).

11. Francis Bacon, *Advancement of Learning*, in *Francis Bacon: Selected Philosophical Works*, ed. Rose-Mary Sargent (Indianapolis: Hackett, 1999), 53–54.

CHAPTER 8

1. The account presented here is based on the recollections of Ira Harkavy, who was "present at the creation," and Martin Blank, the coalition's director, as well as on Blank's "Reaching Out to Create a Movement," in *Community Schools in Action: Learning from a Decade of Practice*, ed. Joy Dryfoos, Jane Quinn, and Carol Barkin (New York: Oxford University Press, 2005), 243–58.

2. Atelia Melaville, *Community Schools: Partnerships for Excellence* (Washington, DC: Coalition for Community Schools, 2000), http://www.communityschools.org/partnerships.html.

3. Ibid.; the quotation is from Frank J. Manley, Bernard W. Reed, and Robert K. Burns, *The Community School in Action: The Flint Program* (Chicago: Education-Industry Service, 1961).

4. Ibid.

5. For a description of the bill, see Full Service Community School Act H.R. 4585.

6. Specifically, the media release issued on June 15, 2004 has statements of support from Ira Harkavy; Joy Dryfoos; Paul Houston, Executive Director of the American Association of School Administrators; Phillip Coltoff, CEO of the Children's Aid Society; and Bill Milliken, founder of Communities in Schools.

7. John Dewey, *Democracy and Education*, in *The Middle Works of John Dewey, 1899–1924*, vol. 9, ed. Jo Ann Boydston (Carbondale: Southern Illinois University Press, 1978), 222. Quotations from *Middle Works* were verified in Larry Hickman, ed., *The Collected Works of John Dewey, 1882–1953: The Electronic Edition* (Charlottesville, VA: InteLex Corporation, 1996).

Index

■ ■
■ ■ About the Authors

Lee Benson is Emeritus Professor of History, University of Pennsylvania.

Ira Harkavy is Associate Vice President and Director of the Center for Community Partnerships, University of Pennsylvania.

John Puckett is Associate Professor in the Policy, Management, and Evaluation Division of the University of Pennsylvania Graduate School of Education. He is the co-author of *Leonard Covello and the Making of Benjamin Franklin High School: Education as if Citizenship Mattered* (Temple).